TEACHABLE MOMENTS

TEACHABLE MOMENTS

The art of teaching in primary schools

Peter Woods and Bob Jeffrey

OPEN UNIVERSITY PRESS
Buckingham · Philadelphia

Open University Press
Celtic Court
22 Ballmoor
Buckingham
MK18 1XW

and
1900 Frost Road, Suite 101
Bristol, PA 19007, USA

First Published 1996

A catalogue record of this book is available from the British Library

ISBN 0 335 19373 0 (pb) 0 335 19374 9 (hb)

Library of Congress Cataloging-in-Publication Data
Woods, Peter.
Teachable moments : the art of teaching in primary schools /
Peter Woods and Bob Jeffrey.
p. cm.
Includes bibliographical references and indexes.
ISBN 0–335–19374–9 (hb). — ISBN 0–335–19373–0 (pb)
1. Elementary school teaching—Great Britain. I. Jeffrey, Bob,
1946– . II. Title.
LB1555.W847 1996
372.11'02—dc20
95–32049   CIP

Typeset by Graphicraft Typesetters Ltd, Hong Kong
Printed in Great Britain by St Edmundsbury Press Ltd,
Bury St Edmunds, Suffolk

To
Bobbie and Lisbeth
and
Kathleen and Elisabeth

Theresa spoke of how she moved from tiredness to active involvement, and when asked what drove her, she answered 'enthusiasm'. Not the enthusiasm of the individual teacher, but of the situation, the context of the children and teacher together which increased the adrenalin. She was swept along by 'the good times'.

(Field note)

CONTENTS

PREFACE

This book is the fourth in a series on the subject of creative teaching. *Teacher Skills and Strategies* (Woods 1990) identified the phenomenon and located it on a range of teacher behaviours that stretched from creative teaching at one end to the practice of survival strategies at the other. *Critical Events in Teaching and Learning* (Woods 1993) explored in detail some exceptional events, mainly in primary schools, which involved and inspired considerable creativity in teacher and pupil alike, and instigated radical educational change and development. The question was then raised as to how this kind of teaching was being affected by the legislation of the late 1980s and early 1990s, which sought a radical reorganization of the education system, and instituted a prescribed National Curriculum. Consequently, *Creative Teachers in Primary Schools* (Woods 1995) examined the reactions of primary teachers to the National Curriculum, showing a range of adaptations from resistance and appropriation to enrichment and re-routeing. A predominant theme throughout, whatever the adaptation, was self-determination: the resolve of teachers to keep faith with their principles and beliefs, to stay true to their own selves, and to seek opportunities for self-renewal and self-realization in – and in some instances out – of teaching.

These have been hard years for teachers, but as one of our sample told us, they have been sustained by 'the good times' or what another called 'teachable moments'. The 'good times' are high moments of successful teaching, fully endorsed by the rewards of pupil accomplishment, often of a radical and unexpected order. Creative teaching has survived, and we return in this book to exploring its nature. What does it consist of? What does it look like? How is it delivered? Why should it be worthy of our attention? What effect does it have on pupils? Does it promote creative learning? This time our concern is not with special events, but with everyday, moment-to-moment classroom matters. We have been interested to see how the deep-seated changes initiated by the 1988 Education Reform Act translate into creative teachers' practice, how teachers handle conflict and opposition, how they generate the conditions conducive to their art. We were also interested to see how teachers handled government attempts to influence teaching method. Until recently, this has been a closed door to central government. They had assumed control of the curriculum in 1988, but how it was to be delivered was still, at that time, regarded as the area of the teacher's professionalism. Soon, however, it came to be realized that method and process was just as important as content and structure. A major initiative was launched, culminating in a document (Alexander *et al.* 1992) which sought to set in train a radical reappraisal of the child-centred ideology most closely associated with the Plowden Report (1967). To some, it seemed that this heralded a return to more traditional, formal approaches. It seemed appropriate, therefore, for us to consider how teachers reacted to these interventions. For reasons of space, this aspect is considered elsewhere (Woods and Wenham 1994).

Creative teaching is not a type of practice employed by a few, special, charismatic teachers constituting some kind of élite among the profession as a whole. Nor do we wish to place teachers in categories. Some of our teachers showed a mix of characteristics, as we discuss in Chapter 2. Creative teaching is not a style; it is, rather, a quality typical of English primary schools over the last generation; it has been practised by many primary teachers to some degree or other, in some form or other. Halliwell (1993) argues that there is a sense in which each act of teaching is a creative act. This may be true, but, on the other hand, teachers cannot always be creative, and opportunities may be becoming fewer. Without falling into the trap of idealizing the past, we have sought to identify some of the prominent features of creative teaching while it is still there to study. Education is still in a state of flux and transition following the 1988 Education Reform Act and other changes of the late 1980s and early 1990s. It is impossible to forecast the future, though the initial radicalism of the legislation appears to be becoming modified, and the moral panics generated during its introduction seem to be abating. Creative teaching may well survive, in which case this book may serve as a guide to some of the features of a sophisticated, interesting and uncommonly productive approach, rather than as a record of what, in some circles, might be regarded as inappropriate and outdated practice. 'The good times' and those 'teachable moments', we hope, are here to stay.

ACKNOWLEDGEMENTS

We would like to thank all the teachers and pupils who took part in the research upon which this book is based. We are especially grateful to Freda, Judy, Mary, Rolf, Sue, Tricia and Val. These were the teachers who were key informers, whose work came to be the chief focus of our attention, and whose testimony guided our enquiry. Their kind of teaching has won an international reputation for English primary schools, but is in danger of being dampened before ever being fully explored and appreciated. We hope we have done justice to their work, though we are able to cover only a small proportion of it here.

We have benefited from many discussions with our colleagues on the Creative Teaching research team, Peter Wenham and Geoff Troman. Peter was involved in the earlier stages of the research, and did much to help us explore the ground, identify possibilities and establish the research on a firm basis. Geoff has contributed to the later stages, and we have gained from the breadth of his sociological knowledge in our analysis. Many others have contributed in various ways: commenting on drafts of articles, responding to conference papers, corresponding or discussing. None of these will necessarily agree with all we have written, but we have learnt a great deal from them. We have received valuable secretarial services from Lynn Tilbury and Aileen Cousins.

Some of the material here has appeared elsewhere in different forms: Chapter 3 in P. Woods (ed.) (1996) *Contemporary Issues in Teaching and Learning*, London, Routledge and Chapter 5 in R. Chawla-Duggan and C. Pole (eds) (1995) *Reshaping Education in the 1990s: Perspectives on Primary Schooling*, London, Falmer Press. Chapter 7 was given as a symposium paper at the annual conference of The British Education Research Association, Oxford, September 1994.

The research for this book was conducted with the aid of grants from the ESRC, award number R000 23 3194, and the Open University. We are grateful to these institutions for their support.

1

CREATIVE TEACHING AND ITS SIGNIFICANCE

The related volume to this book (Woods 1995) discussed, firstly, how English primary schools contrasted strongly with the grim picture of teaching portrayed by Willard Waller (1932) in a text that has influenced conceptions of teaching for over half a century. We now know that picture of Waller's to be *one* of the realities, but only one of the many that can be represented of the complex art of teaching.

Secondly, it noted how, in recent years, teachers' work was being redefined, in danger of becoming a less reflective, thinking activity, in a general drift toward deprofessionalization, de-skilling and intensification (Apple 1986). Initial reactions to the National Curriculum appeared to confirm this process, with teachers experiencing great problems in managing the sheer quantity of prescribed content, and being submerged under the accompanying escalating bureaucratic apparatus (Campbell 1993a). Pollard *et al.* (1994) reported a tendency toward more managerial and directed, as opposed to collegial and participatory, approaches; toward discontinuity with previous practice (p. 75); toward some teachers feeling less creative (p. 85) and showing a shift from expressive to instrumental commitment, and becoming de-skilled (about 50 per cent by 1992 – p. 86); though about 20 per cent thought the National Curriculum enhanced their skills and provided them with opportunities. On the whole, Pollard *et al.* concluded that the picture at the time of their research was unfinished and confused, one that revealed 'change and resistance, commitment and demoralization, decreasing autonomy but some developments in professional skills' (p. 239).

Most teachers, it seems, have viewed the National Curriculum as a hard test of their skills and powers of coping and appropriating. Consequently, thirdly, teachers' creativity in strategic adaptation was examined. Teachers were finding ways of implementing new policies more in line with their own values and beliefs and preferred practices, as they have done in other instances over the years (Ball and Bowe 1992; Osborn and Broadfoot 1992; Vulliamy and Webb 1993). As is so often the case, therefore, it is not a matter of either creativity *or* control, but rather of negotiating a path between them in a varying situation of constraint *and* opportunity. In some situations, the constraint can be severe, and it cannot be denied that there have been profound changes generally in teachers' work across a wide range of activities to do with, for example, curriculum, assessment, role, organization, and conditions (Pollard *et al.* 1994). But we suspected that, as McNamara (1990: 233) puts it, 'the National Curriculum does not present the teaching profession with a non-negotiable set of constraints and given requirements . . . It remains possible for professional teachers to exercise their critical judgement . . . and still remain committed to their own educational values and beliefs.' By concentrating on particularly creative teachers in established situations, we sought to maximize the chances of discovering considerable opportunity and adaptation.

In researching creative teaching, like Halliwell (1993) we have not been concerned with uncommon genius. Nor do we take a psychological view of creativity which locates the basic explanation of creativity within the cognitive domain – the 'golden nugget theory of artistic genius', as Nochlin described it in 1971 (quoted in Gilmore 1990: 153). There are biographical, situational, institutional, structural, resource and relational factors that go into the social production of creative teaching. Unlike Halliwell, however, we *have* been concerned with self-actualization, but not to the extent, certainly, that it becomes self-indulgence and blots out pupil actualization. We also differ from Halliwell in that we are concerned with aesthetic and artistic creativity, not in the limited sense of wall displays and fancy worksheets, but in a more general sense whereby we see the whole of teaching as an artistic accomplishment. Since this perception is basic to what follows, we shall say a little bit more about it here.

TEACHING AS ART

Teaching consists of multiple forms of understanding and representation (Eisner 1993). It is not just a matter of scientific rationality or cognition in words. Abbs (1989) refers to 'our quite remarkable abilities to sequence narratives, to construe analogically, to conceive figuratively, to consider tonally, to think musically, to construct maps and diagrams, to make signs and symbols with our bodies'. Indeed, at times, an important part of teaching is 'not knowing'. For example, to explain might kill the effect of a poem, which requires the imagination to roam free. The art of teaching here lies in the teacher's judgement in circumstances where there is no 'right answer' (Tripp 1993), and where we 'get to know' through all our senses, not just mind.

The teacher's art is expressed through performance. The curriculum is the main vehicle for this, but the curriculum is not a thing or course of study, it is a 'complicated and continual process of environmental design . . . a symbolic, material, and human environment that is ongoingly reconstructed . . . If curriculum is in fact a design problem, then by its very nature it is an aesthetic act. In many ways it is more like painting a picture than building a bridge' (Apple 1993: 144). Carr (1989: 5), discussing the work of Schwab (1969), elaborates further on what is involved in performance:

> Teaching is primarily a 'practical' rather than a 'technical' activity, involving a constant flow of problematic situations which require teachers to make judgements about how best to transfer their general educational values . . . into classroom practice. Interpreted in the language of the 'practical', 'teaching quality' would have little to do with the skilful application of technical rules but instead would relate to the capacity to bring abstract ethical values to bear on concrete educational practice – a capacity which teachers display in their knowledge of what, educationally, is required in a particular situation and their willingness to act so that this knowledge can take a practical form.

This is similar to Eisner's (1985) point about 'connoisseurship'. For Eisner, educational improvement comes not from the discovery of scientific methods that can be applied universally, or from particular personalities, but 'rather from enabling teachers . . . to improve their ability to see and think about what they do' (p. 104), or in other words, their art of appreciation, a subtle ability to discriminate. This contributes to what Polanyi and Prosch (1975) describe as tacitly held practical conduct knowledge, or what Tripp (1993: 129) calls 'practical professionalism'. Tripp contrasts this with scientifically verified knowledge, which is still important, but cannot account for the expertise of all successful teachers. He writes, 'Is this not expertise which comes from intuition, experience and "right-mindedness" rather than scholarly disciplinary knowledge?' (p. 128). Such teaching is expressive and emergent, and cannot be set up in advance through, for example, objectives. Some situations may call for this, but employed as a general framework it forecloses on so many possibilities and opportunities for educational advancement. Teaching requires ends to be created in process, in the 'course of interaction with students rather than preconceived and efficiently attained' (Eisner 1979: 154).

This is why teachers' almost instinctive judgement or intuition is so important. Jackson (1992) does not recognize Waller's description of teaching. He is convinced that teaching has made a big difference in his and in others' lives. He cannot verify this against some external reality or conventional indicators. In considering what teaching has done for him, Jackson relies not on scientific evidence, but on intuition, what feels right to him. This is far from being a matter of guesswork, and involves a host of factors to do with such things as principles, knowledge, and experiences. It is to do, in short, with the sort of person he has become. It is clear that this is one with distinct artistic leanings. We have much to learn, he feels, from the Romantics:

> They constantly sought to look past the world or through it, to see beyond the surface meaning of things. They strove to 'read' their surroundings much as one might read a complicated text or a piece of scripture. Lovers of nature they certainly were, but they also worshipped the human imagination, whose power to envision more than the eye alone could behold was looked upon as the ultimate source of artistic achievement.
>
> (p. 85)

Jackson notes that we must guard against excessive sentimentality, just as against Waller's extreme cynicism and despair. If we think in terms of the sort of person we wish to be and the kind of life we wish to lead, scientific objectivity is completely the wrong approach. What is needed is 'something more like a kindly bias, a forgiving eye, an attitude of appreciation, a way of looking that promotes the growth of sympathetic understanding' (p. 88). We must look at the minutiae of school life through an interpretative frame, cultivating 'a heightened sensitivity to the nuances of schooling' (p. 90). These may involve the way a lesson unfolds, how a teacher constructs a sentence (Highet 1951), creates atmosphere, orchestrates conflicting elements in her role (Lieberman and Miller 1984; Woods 1990), balances priorities, dilemmas, pressures, and her own aims through exercising a complex and demanding skill (Nias 1989), involves her whole self and her pupils likewise in situations where they realize their full identity – all of this involves teachers giving an 'aesthetic form to their existence through their own productive work' (Foucault 1979).

Jackson's approach acknowledges the emotional heart of teaching. A. Hargreaves (1994) represents this as 'desire', which is

> imbued with 'creative unpredictability' and 'flows of energy' . . . In desire is to be found the creativity and spontaneity that connects teachers emotionally . . . to their children, their colleagues and their work. Such desires among particularly creative teachers are for fulfilment, intense achievement, senses of breakthrough, closeness to fellow humans, even love for them . . . Without desire, teaching becomes arid and empty. It loses its meaning.
>
> (p. 22)

Teaching is not a mechanical exercise. As Highet (1951: viii) argues, 'you must throw your heart into it'. Some find it difficult to talk dispassionately about teaching (for example, Rogers 1983). This does not mean that the use of emotion is completely undisciplined and unchannelled, clarity and guidance is needed (Collingwood 1966). Emotion is also a subject of development as well as a means of motivation and contextualization. Students' emotional development through drama, through narrative and story, through relationships, and the general ethos of classroom and school is a matter of prime concern.

The emotions are also important for cognition. Mackey (1993: 250) argues that 'there are occasions when the emotions cause the senses to be heightened such that sights, sounds, smells, tastes and the tactile send stronger images to the brain . . . Our grasp on the real world is deepened by the intensity of these images.' She gives examples from her own experience, similar to what D. Hargreaves (1983) calls 'conversive traumas' – cathartic experiences undergone in appreciating works of art, not unlike religious conversions. These can lead to motivation for more similar experiences, and for more knowledge within which to contextualize the trauma.

Artistic teaching takes risks and potentially breaks rules. It can question 'the boundaries of our existence' (Bolton 1994: 95). Exploration involves freedom to try out new ways, new activities, different solutions, some of which will inevitably fail. It is important that education provides that kind of opportunity and disposition to play, and to take it to the limit, for 'to be able to play with ideas is to feel free to throw them into new combinations, to experiment, and even "to fail"' (Eisner 1979: 160). Play stimulates the educational imagination and increases the ability to see and take advantage of new opportunities.

This is not to say that in some important respects, teaching is not a science, nor that the scientific study of teaching has not much to offer – indeed, we would claim that our own approach is scientific in several ways, for example in its concern for validity, and in trying to identify general properties. But it would appear that the artistic side of teaching has been, and is in danger of becoming even more, undervalued.

THE NEED FOR CREATIVE TEACHING

Teaching needs to be creative for the following reasons:

1   Every situation is different. A multiplicity of factors affect the teaching moment involving such shifting elements as the state of knowledge, space and time, cultural considerations, resources, human capacity and predilection. As Dewey (1929: 6) notes, 'Judgement and belief regarding actions to be performed can never attain more than a precarious probability . . . Practical activity deals with individualized and unique situations which are never exactly duplicable and about which, accordingly, no complete

assurance is possible.' Only so much is predictable. There is a need, there-fore, for teachers to be flexible. It is not a matter of having certain fixed solutions that can be applied to certain fixed problems; nor of reflecting on the possibilities and making a conscious decision about which com-bination of actions to take. Rather, skill and judgement are required in selecting from and applying existing knowledge in what Schön (1983) calls 'knowledge-in-action'. Much of this is embedded deep within the teacher's subconscious, and operated intuitively. Teachers may find it difficult to articulate in words the reasons for their actions, but this is typical of artistic accomplishments (Hargreaves 1983).

2 There has been a proliferation of new policy which threatens to in-tensify teachers' work and disempower them. As Ball (1994: 19; see also Riseborough 1992) points out, it cannot be taken for granted that policy is simply applied, for it has to be interpreted on the ground and *in situ*:

> Responses must be 'creative' . . . Given constraints, circumstances and practicalities, the translation of the crude, abstract simplicities of policy texts into interactive and sustainable practices of some sort involves productive thought, invention and adaptation. Policies . . . create cir-cumstances in which the range of options available in deciding what to do are narrowed or changed, or particular goals or outcomes are set . . . All of this involves creative social action, not robotic reactivity.

The point applies in a more general sense, for it is likely that teacher cul-ture will be undergoing profound change (D. Hargreaves 1994). As McCall and Wittner (1990: 58) observe, 'Given new conditions, people invent cul-ture'. Chapter 3 discusses this at further length.

3 Tensions and dilemmas in teaching are proliferating. Berlak and Berlak (1981) showed how teachers are constantly, in their everyday practice, wrest-ling with a number of dilemmas, often contemporaneously, and having to make decisions about them. Some of these are: when to teach individual children and when the whole class? When to make decisions for children and when to allow them to make decisions? Whether to put the emphasis on intrinsic or extrinsic motivation? Whether to concentrate on a narrow range of control represented by the child as *student*, or a broader range represented by the *whole* child? In general, teachers would be concerned with how to transform dilemmas into educational chances; how to maxim-ize the possibilities; how to convert what might seem, in some circum-stances, constraints, to what become, in other circumstances, opportunities. There is no single right answer to this kind of problem, but rather, as Tom (1988: 49) notes, 'multiple potential solutions whose effectiveness is largely unknown prior to the act of teaching'. Chapter 7 has a fuller discussion of these points.

4 Teaching is an act of faith, which requires, for many, strong investment of the self. Nias (1989: 182) shows how for most 'to adopt the identity of "teacher" was simply to "be yourself" in the classroom'; and how they 'linked the notions of "being yourself" and "being whole"'. Others have testified how, with this level of commitment, teachers have to feel right in order to perform to full effect (for example, Riseborough 1981). Teachers are not technicians, bland mediators or implementers of others' programmes (Schön 1983; MacIntyre 1984; Olson 1992). Most have strong beliefs and values which are deeply involved in their teaching, and through which the requirements of State, parents, governors, and not least, students, have to be mediated (Ball and Bowe 1992; Vulliamy and Webb 1993). Something of teachers' own selves is transmitted. Teachers need to be creative, therefore, to secure the 'personal touch', to adapt the curriculum so that they can feel a sense of ownership of the knowledge to be transmitted and/or learned, so that they can feel in control of the pedagogical process, and so that they can develop a personal style. We conceive of 'style' here, not in terms of the generalized 'teaching styles' that have featured so prominently in primary school researches, such as in those of Bennett (1976) and in the ORACLE studies (for example, Galton and Simon 1980), but as Hansen (1993: 397) sees it,

> a set of habits that includes gestures, body movements, facial expressions and tones of voice. The term encompasses a teacher's customary ways of attending to students, for example how he or she typically responds to what they say and do ... these habits or elements of working style, reflect more than personality as well as more than conventional or instrumental behaviour. They can be seen to reveal the interest, the involvement, the expectations that guide the teacher's efforts.

These expressive dimensions of a teacher's conduct, especially in the minutiae of classroom life, which are often overlooked because they appear trivial and mundane, exert considerable moral influence on students (p. 418). Chapters 4 and 5 develop these ideas more fully.

5 Students require creative teaching, in at least two ways. Much learning is a gradual, slowly cumulative process, but sometimes there are extraordinary leaps (Hargreaves 1983; Woods 1994). Totally unexpected opportunities to secure an advance in a pupil's learning may occur. There is a need to recognize these when we see them, for they may be transient and not occur again; a need to know how to grasp the opportunity and to maximize gain; a need, too, to know how to construct situations so that opportunities have a chance to happen. This may mean 'ringing the changes' in order to find 'ways in' to children so that they can 'break out' – common terms used among primary teachers in describing their practice.

The second way derives from the fact that students are not just flesh and blood, but also emotional and cultural beings. They need to relate to what is taught, to recognize its relevance to their concerns, to have their imaginations stimulated, to feel motivated to learn. In some instances, where situations of basic conflict prevail, teachers and students negotiate a working consensus – an agreement on work rates and sanctions that secures a modicum of returns, but falls somewhat short of inspired teaching and learning (Reynolds 1976; Pollard 1979). To achieve the latter, everyone has to feel right. The school day has to be tinctured with feelings of excitement, involvement, curiosity, personal identification, being caught up with a group in a shared venture – see especially Chapter 6.

6   The teacher is naturally creative in the view of the general theoretical approach behind the research, that of symbolic interactionism. Plummer (1983: 1–5) points to four central criteria:

> *human subjectivity and creativity* – showing how individuals respond to social constraints and actively assemble social worlds; it must deal with concrete human experiences – talk, feelings, action – through their *social, and especially economic organization* (and not just their inner, psychic and biological structuring); it must show a naturalistic '*intimate familiarity*' with such experiences . . . and there must be a self-awareness by the sociologist of the ultimate *moral and political role* in moving towards a social structure in which there is less exploitation, oppression and injustice, and more creativity, diversity and equality.

Social organization is seen as a negotiated order which emerges as people try to solve the problems they encounter in concrete situations. We ask, therefore, what are the problems teachers face as they see them? How are they experienced, what meanings are given to them and what feelings generated? Finally, how are they resolved? Though there may have been an assault on professional autonomy recently (Hatcher 1994), interactionists look at how people 'carve out autonomy despite their lack of formal power' (McCall and Wittner 1990: 70). The emphasis is upon the construction of meanings and perspectives, the adaptation to circumstances, the management of interests in the ebb and flow of countless interactions containing many ambiguities and conflicts, the strategies devised to promote those interests, and the negotiation with others' interests that is a common feature of all teaching situations (Woods 1992). By definition, this theoretical approach is about creativity, for its subject is the active, thinking, feeling, inventive self in the context of an often unhelpful and obstructive world. In his conceptualization of the self, Mead (1934) distinguished the creative 'I' from the self-regulated and socially controlled 'me'. Novel acts are always emerging from the 'I', often to our own as well as others' astonishment. 'We do not know just what they are. They are in a certain sense the most fascinating contents that we can contemplate' (Mead 1934: 205). Mead argued that the unique creative contributions of the individual were the most precious qualities of the individual, both for the individual and for society.

There have been few studies of the 'I', partly because the predilection for conflict and constraints research has directed attention toward the 'me', partly because the 'I' is so elusive. As soon as one reflects, the 'I' becomes part of the 'me'. But it is important as it is a way of conceptualizing a degree of personal autonomy against the forces of social conditioning. Nias (1989) has given some prominence to this aspect, exploring what it feels like to be a primary school teacher, which includes emotional, and, at times, unruly and irrational behaviour. We investigate the activity of the 'I' in relation to specific teaching tasks, the emotional aspects being a particular concern – see especially Chapter 4.

7 There is a need for *genuine* creativity. There have been failed attempts. King (1978) noted how teachers partly organized pupils' creative work to reproduce conventional or orthodox reality, and how teachers' creative public displays were often at the expense of pupils' learning. Further, they 'defined children's creative work as being an expression of their development, and acted in such a way as to make the nature of their creative products correspond to the presumed stages of development' (quoted in Bourne 1994: 228). Similarly, a number of reputedly creative teaching approaches have been shown to be nothing of the sort (see, for example, Atkinson and Delamont 1977; Edwards and Furlong 1978). More recently, child-centred progressivism, which has been so influential in primary schools over the past 30 years, has come under attack. Alexander (1992: 169) noted the strength and influence of this ideology in the Leeds primary schools of his research. He observed that 'properly to belong one needed to accept and enact the ideology, and that mechanisms existed to encourage such acceptance' (p. 169). By the late 1980s, it was 'an ideology grounded in the best of intentions which for many has lost its early intellectual excitement and has become a mere shell of slogans and procedures, sometimes adopted for no other reason than the desire or need to conform' (p. 194). It had bred a range of 'sacred cows and shibboleths', such as 'enquiry methods', integration, resistance to subjects; and slogans, such as 'we teach children, not subjects', 'learning how to learn, rather than what to learn', 'discovery, not instruction'. This would appear to be a good example of how an ideology, purporting to have an opposite effect, can operate as a constraint. However, whatever the circumstances in the Leeds primary schools, the teachers of our research still exhibited intellectual, moral and emotional excitement over what they understood to be child-centred education, practised in the detailed, personal way described above, and were alive to the possibilities of its abuse.

RESEARCH METHODS

Given our view of the unpredictable nature of teaching and the seren-
dipitous elements that attend its success, like Tom (1988: 49), we believe
that 'we can recognize teaching effectiveness, if at all, only *after* the fact.'
In our quest, therefore, to understand the nature of creative teaching
further, we sought out teachers who seemed to exemplify in abund-
ance the qualities previously identified. These qualities were manifested
in their general behaviour, teaching activities, outlook, language, relationships and results. It was then a matter of observing their teaching in some
detail, and discussing with them their practice and the principles behind
it. We regarded these teachers, in other words, as 'critical cases'. The principle is one of 'theoretical representativeness', leading to 'judgement sampling' (Johnson 1990: 28). The criteria for selection were not objective
in terms of some clear-cut factor such as age, sex or subject taught, but
based on a judgement about how far a teacher met the criteria adopted
(innovative teaching, ownership of knowledge, control of pedagogy, relevance of values). As well as the theoretical criteria, there were opera-
tional ones concerning matters like willingness to engage in the research,
amount of time prepared to give to it, the potential for developing trust
and rapport with the researchers, and the teachers' articulateness.

The sample was identified by an initial trawl of schools in the two areas
of the research, London and one of the Home Counties, among personal
contacts and through official channels. From this, we selected a number
of teachers – about 20 in each area – who assisted us in the early stages
as we investigated reactions to the National Curriculum and how it had
affected their teaching, and sought to identify any general themes or
issues. As we came to focus in on particular issues as guided by the accu-
mulating data, we increasingly came to rely on fewer key informants. Thus,
the material in the book is largely, though not entirely, based on research
done with seven teachers. We shall say more about the most prominent
three of these teachers in Chapter 2. We cannot claim that they are representative of teachers as a whole, or of creative teachers as a particular
category – whatever that might be. There are a variety of value positions
among teachers, inducing different reactions to the National Curriculum
(see, for example, Mac an Ghaill 1992), and probably generational differences linked with position in the career structure. New teachers trained
in the National Curriculum might be expected to react differently from
those nearing retirement. In these terms, we considered our sample a
key group – in mid-career, experienced, well respected, generally highly
regarded by their peers, pupils' parents and inspectors (in the past) as
successful, and with management as well as teaching responsibilities. In
the end, however, representativeness is not the issue. We would turn the
point round, suggesting that what these teachers say and do is of especial

Figure 1.1

School and teachers		Years experience	Age	Post
Inchmery	Theresa	20+	40–50	DH
	Wendy	15+	30–40	2PTS
	Thea	10+	30–40	2PTS
	Winsome	15+	30–40	2PTS
	Terrie	1	20–30	
	William	10+	30–40	2PTS
Cantor	Eddie	15+	40–50	DH
	Nicola	5+	30–40	P/T support
	Erica	15+	30–40	P/T support
	Eve	1	20–30	
	Nadine	5+	20–30	1PT
	Nathan	3+	20–30	2PTS
	Norma	15+	40+	2PTS
	Esther	15+	40–50	1PT
Sleek	Grace	20+	40–50	DH
Livery	Laura	10+	40–50	2PTS
Girthwaite	Marilyn	15+	40–50	2PTS
Mane	Sandra	10+	30–40	1PT
Forelock	Peter	15+	30–40	DH
Harness	Andrea	10+	30–40	2PTS

PTS = extra points on the Teachers' Main Grade Scale for areas of responsibility
DH = deputy head
P/T = part-time support. Some of this may have been Section 11 work with pupils whose parents were from New Commonwealth countries

interest, and others might consider how representative their teaching is – or should be. Details of the teachers and schools involved in the research are given in Figures 1.1 and 1.2. All names used are pseudonyms.

The research began in January, 1992, and ran, in the first instance, for two years. At a late stage, funds were secured for an extra year to complete the work upon which Chapters 2 to 7 are based. Data collection was through qualitative methods, consisting chiefly of interviews and classroom observation, but including a range of other methods as occasion demanded, such as the use of documents and photography. These interconnected and extended, and facilitated triangulation. Interviews were informal affairs. We saw them as processes involving pre- and post-interview strategies and reflection, connecting with other discussions and conversations with the same person, together with observation of their work in a seamless web of methods designed to reconstruct the nature of their work. We aimed to generate theory from the data using the process of constant comparative analysis (Glaser and Strauss 1967; Strauss and Corbin 1990). By comparing transcripts and field notes both within and

Figure 1.2

There are five main schools used for the focused study. All five schools were State-maintained non-denominational schools, in mainly working-class areas. However, one school – Inchmery – had approximately 20–30 per cent of its pupils from more professional white-collar backgrounds.

School	Location	Type	Intake	Size
Cantor	Inner city	Purpose-built one-level 1970s	Mixed. Majority intake Bangladeshi	One-form entry
Sleek	Inner city	Victorian three-decker	Mixed. Majority intake Afro-Caribbean and minority Vietnamese	Three-form entry
Livery	Inner city	Victorian three-decker	Mixed. Majority intake Afro-Caribbean	One-form entry
Girthwaite	Suburban estate	Purpose-built two-level 1980s	Majority: white. Approx. 10 per cent ethnic minorities	One-form entry
Inchmery	Inner city	Victorian three-decker	Mixed. 30–40 per cent ethnic minorities	One-form entry

across cases, we were able to identify issues and themes, which then guided a new round of data collection in a spiral of method development (Lacey 1976).

An additional feature of the research was the extent of collaboration sought with the teachers and schools concerned. We wished to do research with teachers, rather than on them. This was for a number of reasons. Firstly, it seemed ethically appropriate, given that we were working so closely with these teachers for such a long period in their schools, that we viewed them as highly skilled and accomplished professionals, and that they had a vital interest in the outcomes of the research which bore on their work. Secondly, the teachers, represented a resource with particular knowledge, skills and insight, that could be put into the research in a way that was different from us, the researchers, but that was just as valuable in its own right. Thirdly, we see a major purpose of our research as feeding back into schools and teaching, and we feel this needs to be carried out through teachers if it is to have any effect. Our teachers are sharing their views and experiences not only with us, but with their fellow professionals elsewhere, for them to discuss and incorporate into their own perspectives and cultures (Fullan 1992). Fourthly, like critical theorists (Gitlin 1990;

Smyth 1991; Kincheloe 1993), we are opposed to élitist, hierarchical forms of research which exploit subjects for academics' own benefit. We were conscious of what Fine (1994) describes as 'othering' – seeing teachers as completely separate and different from us. A fifth, and related, point, is that we were only too conscious that we were two males (three in the earlier stages) researching an area overwhelmingly staffed by women. One way in which we could seek to compensate for this was by co-opting the (mainly women) teachers on to the research. Another was by ensuring that the point was a regular item on the agendas of our research meetings, together with reflection on possible influences on the research. We hope to discuss this, and other methodological issues, at greater length in later research papers.

We have given one example of how collaboration worked, in relation to the teaching and researching of a history project, in previous material (Woods and Wenham 1994; Woods 1995). However, the collaboration did not always work as well as this for two main reasons. One was the traditional perception of teacher and researcher roles; the other was the pressures of workload the teachers were under. The latter has inhibited the very basis of qualitative research, such as gaining access, never mind thoughts of extending techniques such as collaboration (Troman 1996). It makes it difficult to make inroads on the traditional perception, unless it contributes to easing the pressures, as the history project did. None the less, we tried as far as possible to promote joint research, feeding back drafts of papers for comment, holding seminars and contributing to inservice days, assuming the role of researcher-teacher and assisting teachers in their work, thus mirroring the role extended to them – that of teacher-researcher. The liberal use of transcript in the text, within the conventional constraints of book production, is in recognition of the fact that teachers are best placed to tell their own stories, and that these stories are, in fact, the life-blood of their teaching, its moral foundation (Olson 1992). As Smyth (1995: 82) argues, 'We need to watch and listen to the ways in which teachers themselves seek to attach significance to what it is they do, and how they individually and collectively struggle to contest and redefine the work of schooling.' Furthermore, teachers 'need to be more forceful than they have been in the past at trumpeting the virtues of what is happening in schools and classrooms' (pp. 85–6; see also Clark 1992). This book is part of that endeavour.

2

CREATIVE TEACHERS

In this chapter, we introduce some of the chief participants upon whose practice the analysis of creative teaching is largely based. We shall say something about their values and interests, their feelings and anxieties, and the content and style of their teaching. In previous accounts, we have depicted creative teachers as being innovative, having ownership of the knowledge and being in control of the teaching processes involved, and operating within a broad range of accepted social values while being attuned to pupil cultures (Woods 1990, 1995). We have argued that this produces higher-order teaching and learning (see also Woods 1993). In this chapter, we select a representative three teachers from our main sample to concentrate on in order to illustrate some of the differences and similarities among them and to extend the discussion of creative teaching attributes.

All three were over 40 years of age. They worked in Victorian three-decker inner-city schools and taught a class full time. All were part of the senior management team in their schools. We are introduced to them here by some of their colleagues and parents. We then look at differences between them before considering their similarities.

Grace

Grace was deputy head of a large inner-city 600-pupil school with about 20 years' experience of teaching. She taught mainly infants in her early years but had taught juniors for the previous five years. Helen, another experienced teacher, worked with Grace as a part-time support teacher and here she talks about how she saw Grace as a teacher.

> They [the children] are very much aware of Grace at all times and they are relating directly to her. In other classes I go in the children are aware of the teacher when she's in front of them but they are not

quite so with the teacher the whole time. Each child in Grace's class seems to be with her like in a one-to-one situation . . . They're bees round a honey pot. They want to please her and make sure they do everything right. They're all working in order to attain that. They describe her as a strict teacher, and they see that as a good thing and they all do what Grace wants and that's a positive thing . . . because the work is there to show it . . . when she says something nice about them, they absolutely love it. They really feel good about themselves. That's better than all the treats . . . So they want to please her and to work well. It encourages them all with the same aim to do well . . . she really does know how to make people feel good about themselves, how to make them feel valued.

Theresa

Theresa had also taught for more than 20 years, mostly in secondary schools. She transferred to primary after completing an MA in technology and now worked as deputy head in an expanding one-form inner-city school with a varied class and ethnic population. A field note records a parent's view of Theresa. The parent worked voluntarily in the class for two mornings a week.

She described Theresa as a strong character with a flexible approach. Theresa was dedicated and strict, a strong planner who thought out her plans carefully but who was able to be spontaneous. She ensured that activities were geared to children's levels – a considerable accomplishment. Theresa knew the children well. She knew their home background and their character faults. She was interested in them as people and saw how they related to each other and was aware of their emotional problems. The parent liked the fact that Theresa knew her child and commented on her. Theresa had described her daughter as internally anxious and the parent was glad that Theresa had spotted this before the parent mentioned it. [i.e. she was skilful in understanding children as well as giving time to them.] There was a habit of work in the classroom and the parent saw Theresa as wanting to get the best out of her pupils. She noted that Theresa doesn't give up easily. They know they will be 'pounced upon'. [This is interpreted to mean that she will not accept shoddy work and this is confirmed by her children.] The parent's view was that one can't teach by fear but the pupils know what to expect if they under-achieve. The parent's opinion was that some children will get away with murder if they are allowed to. The parent was grateful that her child had Theresa as a teacher because of her enthusiasm and how she got her daughter to work. 'Getting her to work gives her confidence.' The parent believed that Theresa got the children to believe that they 'could do it'. However she also noted Theresa's concern for their dignity. For example, Theresa set targets but didn't show the children up if they hadn't achieved them.

The observation that she doesn't give up easily is confirmed by one of her children:

> I think that she's got a good sense of humour because when she's talking to you she sort of understands you, and if you sort of don't understand it, she just doesn't sort of, give up like sometimes your mum and dad do if you do work for them, they go 'Oh I give up.' But with Theresa she carries on listening to you and carries on even if it takes all day.

As with Grace, there is a clear indication of a teacher who was quite in control, who planned in depth, expected high standards and was also sensitive to pupils' relations with their work.

Laura

After a ten-year break from teaching, Laura had been teaching for the last five years in an inner-city school. At the time of the research, she had a Year 2 class. Again, a parent who worked with Laura a few days a week gives her opinion.

> I think children like Laura. I think that is because when they go in other classes they come back and they say, 'Oh, that teacher shouts so much and Laura doesn't shout'. And I think she gives the same amount of attention, well almost, to all the children, I don't think any feel left out and she values all their work, whether someone's written half a line or someone's written two pages she gives them the same encouragement. I think it must be hard because they could all be writing about the same thing but there are so many different levels in the class yet she still seems to get something out of all of them . . . And also I like a lot of the art work that she does. I think she's been to art school . . . I don't think there's many 7-year-olds that have been able to print on silk and make cards and things like that. A lot of it starts off as her idea, she wants them to print on silk and yet it's still their work that comes out of it, it's not hers, you know, you can see it's come from them if you see what I mean . . . I've always felt at ease in her classroom. I've only been in one other classroom before and I don't really want to go back there. She makes me feel at ease and I'm not frightened of doing something wrong and getting told to do it differently . . . She's not afraid of being criticized, not that she is very often. I admire her confidence, I suppose, and the fact that she gets results.

DIFFERENCES

Creative teachers are not all alike, nor are they always being creative. Subjectivities and identities are constructed in multilayered and contradictory ways (Davies and Harré 1990). Identity is not only a historical and social construction, but is also a process of transformation and change (Giroux 1992). We hope to show, in the course of the book, how multilayered these teachers are and how fundamental this is to their engagement with creative teaching. There are four categories of difference we focus on here: career, performance, confidence and planning.

Career

Laura was a 'career returner'. Her memories of her earlier teaching period contrast sharply with her arrival back in the classroom during the year in which the Education Reform Act was passed. The distancing of teacher and children in the first school she worked in seemed to be caused by the introduction of the National Curriculum. In this particular school, she says,

> There seemed to be a change in the power basis in the classroom and the teacher seemed to know everything and they felt they just had to impart it. It seemed that this was happening a lot more. And I felt how rare it seemed to ever hear a teacher say sorry to children. For a start, the teachers were anxious all the time, they were overloaded, they were just trying to take on board what the National Curriculum was all about and not realizing it was totally impossible anyway having new orders after new orders slapped on them. It seemed so dishonest, what was happening between teachers and children. I came to London on a sort of 'welcome back to teaching course', 'pop in for three days and we'll stick you straight in the classroom 'cos you look as though you can handle it.' Some of the things I came in and saw made me think 'What are they doing? This is madness! What are they playing at here? This is not education!'

Within a short while she moved to her present school,

> because in this school I actually felt a different atmosphere to the children and I just felt I understood what the school was doing. They seemed to be doing something that meant something to children. I'm not saying that they weren't also overloaded, they certainly were, but there were enough teachers who were sincere about what they were doing and I found that's what attracted me to the school.

Grace had a more traditional primary experience. She went from school to college, and then straight into infant teaching. She moved once, to her present school as deputy head, though there was an amalgamation in 1990 with the junior school on the same site. She has remained as one of two deputy heads in this large three-form entry school. After the amalgamation she agreed to work in the juniors for the first time in her career, and had done so for the last four years prior to the research.

Theresa had previously been, in her terms, a successful secondary teacher in the arts field who engaged in a number of community projects. However, she became disillusioned with secondary education and, after gaining an MA in technology and being an adviser for a while, she decided she wanted to teach in a primary school. Her first appointment was as deputy head. She had had this post for two years. As Theresa said,

> Walking into those primary schools there was a realization that I had been in secondary schools for years and had the reputation of being this amazingly good teacher and actually being hit by the ball of truth when you walked into a primary school, a very good primary school, by the fact that you had never ever taught in your life. That in fact you were a very good instructor, an amazingly good instructor, but you hadn't ever actually addressed the fact of teaching. And I think, when I went into a primary school, especially as an advisory teacher I met all the people that I had never met at a course. I met all those people who had not been trampling on anybody else's neck to get to the top because they were far too bloody busy doing what they were doing. And the quality of those people, when you meet them for the first time really is like a big shot in the solar plexus, because after 20 years in the secondary school and having to suddenly realize the actuality that you hadn't even begun to address why you were there and you had this massive reputation and you hadn't even done it. And yet little Miss So-and-so who had been in a primary school for 36 years had been doing it every day and no one had noticed.

Performance

They described their teaching style in different ways. Grace and Theresa talked about their teaching style more in terms of performance than Laura. Grace liked 'selling. Persuading them to believe in something that I believed in . . . I'd quite enjoy that . . . that's the kind of challenge that might suit my nature.' 'Selling', rather ironically here, has overtones of either a marketing philosophy or a confidence trick. However, Grace was using common linguistic currency to describe a significant feature of her practice, that of exciting children and being excited herself about their interests. This is the more aesthetic side of the teachers' art and they were aware of its power. As Theresa stated,

> It's emotive, it's dangerous, it's a feeling of power. It could be corruptive if you feed out crap information. It can be magical when it works and there have been times when I've stood up in front of a

class and talked in an electrifying way about salt water and the power of doing that can be intoxicating. You've got to know in the back of your mind what you are doing.

Laura, on the other hand, was a lot less dramatic in her style. She pursued a more conversational style in her class and tried a very open approach. It is a risk-taking activity, for, on occasions, it can lead to a loss of control, but she considered that worth trading for the educational gains:

> You always have a certain amount of tension that comes in a dialogue. Yes, teaching is not always to do with control, because sometimes in the classroom I seem to lose total control because of the lengthy dialogues we engage in, but I just have to think, 'Oh God! Let's try this again, let's go from somewhere else.' Just getting them back together again, it does happen. New teachers think that it doesn't ever happen to other people. They think it's only them who lose their grasp of the class.

However, although she may not be performing like Grace and Theresa, Laura is still orchestrating (Woods 1990) like the other teachers:

> You need to do this for children to accept you as an honest person. There's got to be a feeling of trust. I'm not saying I'm always straight with the kids, sometimes I'm playing at being angry. I mean I'm orchestrating things, definitely, because that's the art of teaching isn't it? Quite often I'm asking children to work in different groups for reasons which I don't always put forward to them . . . it would be too complicated.

These distinctions of performance are also related to some distinctions in classroom control. Theresa and Grace were considered strict in that they played an overtly dominant role in the class. Whole-class sessions were quiet ones where there were formal methods to speak ('hands up'), and only one child spoke at a time on most occasions. An exciting atmosphere was often created with both the use of tone and a broad range of evocative language and variation in the pace of their delivery (see Chapter 5). Their classrooms were filled with attractive displays. However, they also talked of feeling drained by their teaching experience. Theresa thought that the way that she taught was not 'physically or emotionally the easiest way to do it'.

By contrast, Laura spent more time having class discussions. There was more spontaneous input from the children. It was only when the teacher wanted a particular child's comment to be heard that the class was encouraged to be silent. The teacher talked over the comments using her voice to move the discussion on or to highlight particular points. Opinions and less relevant interjections were valued and some hares chased. Arguments

over comments sometimes broke out and the teacher was constantly medi-
ating and chairing the session. The control was negotiated by the teacher
from a position of strength but only rarely imposed. However, this meant
that constant appeals were made by the teacher for order, using a kind of
polite discourse ('excuse me'). The tone Laura adopted to engage pupils
was not so much dramatic as inviting. Her classroom displays were more
'displays in progress', where children added elements as the term progressed, than completed curriculum statements of achievement.

Confidence

The teachers differed in degrees of personal confidence, though all
were well respected by their colleagues. Though both Theresa and Grace
favoured a more teacher-centred approach, they differed in terms of private confidence. Theresa, in conversation, told many stories of her successful past teaching experience and she exuded confidence in terms of
her current practice.

> With me, if you're teaching the arts, everything has got to be worked
> out in terms of practical space, in terms of organizational space, and
> in terms of breaking it down to, in terms of 1, 2, 3, 4, 5, and you can
> go and do it and how! And then reassessing that when it's on the go
> and on the move, thinking on your feet, being quite free to adapt
> what's happening. That's where my strengths are coming from, that's
> where my experience and education comes from . . . Like when we
> started off with those plant drawings. A lot of them really needed to
> feel that they could do it. If you start with this you look for the land-
> mark, you look for the thing that stands out, you build it around it,
> it's like a jigsaw, you put it back together another way. You give them
> all sorts of very practical ways of putting it together, right?

Grace, on the other hand, rarely talked confidently about her teaching,
though she actually looked very confident in the class. Many of her comments were tinged with irony as she disparaged herself. When the researcher complimented her on an aspect of her teaching, she said, 'Then
you're easily impressed'. She said her relationship with children was 'growing negative by the day'. She would not accept that her children were well
behaved. In response to the observation from the researcher that she
established very warm relationships with her children, she remarked
mockingly 'Friends die quickly, Bob'. Sometimes, she felt, 'I've been really
comfortable with them and things are going well, and then other times,
like this morning, I felt, "My God! This is awful!"' She tended to under-
rate her relationship with the children:

> It would be a hell of a lot easier if we enjoy what we do. It comes over
> you, and when I think back ten years ago . . . You couldn't get me out

of school on a Friday, I looked forward to a Monday. I was totally different. When you have that enthusiasm it shows, you perform at a higher level in a much more productive way. So I always feel they know me, kids know, they can pick up everything. Sometimes maybe I'm staring or something, I don't know what I was doing, but they said 'What are you thinking about?' They pick up little flashes of me, maybe, I don't know, being withdrawn or being blank and they pick it up so I often think I can't fool them . . . They're with me all the time. I try to, but I don't think I do. I think they sense my tension and I often think this makes them tense. Sometimes I think I don't get that close to them. I look at other teachers and some teachers have a real closeness with the kids. Mine is never. I don't get that close to many people anyway but certainly not the kids . . . No matter how lovely these kids are I never feel that close to kids. And I think they sense this. They know my insincerity and my distance and my resistance, they can pick all that up.

This description has to be contrasted with her support teacher's view of her and numerous evaluations from her children about how they enjoyed being in her class. Grace was very critical of her practice and it appeared to be very difficult to get her to believe anything different. However, the fact remains that she was highly praised in her school by her colleagues and her pupils.

Grace tells other tales of being criticized and having a low esteem. When she went for the deputy headship, it was the head who persuaded her, and who phoned the inspector and extolled her virtues. She herself felt 'this is madness, I can't do this'. The head told her 'For goodness' sake, Grace! Will you stop putting yourself down and think positively? You've done these things and you've got to say you've done these things.' She went through traumas 'you wouldn't believe' for about three months, losing weight, and sleep: 'The whole thing was negative, and it's never gone away.' There may well be a gender element here. Walkerdine (1989) has pointed to the difficulties some women experience in a patriarchal society in recognizing their own capabilities. This is even more the case in areas of male dominance, such as in higher management in primary schools (Acker 1994).

Laura combined characteristics of both Theresa and Grace, for she saw herself as being arrogant enough to know what was right for children, but at the same time she was anxious about doing the right thing. She had 'a feeling that she knew what children needed'. She could not always 'articulate it, but imagined what they were feeling and related it to things she had felt in the past'. She knew 'good places to take them' and 'good experiences to show them', and felt her experiences much better for these purposes than those of the Secretary of State of the day, for hers 'show people relating in a good way, being more caring and enjoying the life that they have . . . it's the way we've related to other people that's important.' But her anxiety goes 'hand in hand with that'. She worries about the difficulties in her chosen course of action, and she worries about when she is called to account for her actions:

> What am I going to do when OFSTED (the Office for Standards in Education) arrive? How can I explain all this to them? How can I tie this in with the forms that I'm filling in? I'm not sure if it can be done in any better way than paying lip service to what they're asking you to do, but that's not where I want to put the focus of my energy. I'm here with this group of children. I'm seeing what they're doing every day and the problems they have.

Planning

The teachers also varied in their approach to planning. Grace spent a lot of time on planning.

> When I've gone out the night before or I'm so tired and I've just gone home and sat and watched the telly and I'm not prepared, it has an effect on the day. And I know it's not them, I know it's me. Ninety per cent of the time when I've had a bad day, it's me, it's because I've not prepared this, because I haven't given it enough thought.

Grace was admired by other staff for her powerful influential assemblies but she said she refused to do an assembly at short notice.

> If he [the head] asked me the night before, fine, but don't ask me to do it five minutes before because I couldn't do it. I have to feel I've got something, that it's going to be a session that they want to listen to and I'm not shushing children up. I don't want to be standing up in front of 300 children telling them to shush so I would refuse to do it. But some people can do it. They've got the confidence and they can think of something off the top of their head and in they go and do it so wonderfully, I can't do it. After 20 years I still can't do it.

Theresa, on the other hand, called herself a 'fly-by-the-seat-of-your-pants' teacher. She might plan things systematically, but 'I know as soon as it starts coming out of my mouth, it will naturally break down into processes.' The parent mentioned earlier (p. 15) actually thought Theresa's work rigorously planned, and observed that 'sometimes when you come into the room it looks really superb'. But, according to Theresa, the conscious planning may have

> perhaps been ten minutes on the train at the weekend, but what I do feel I have is a very clear overall plan of what I want to get through

during the year . . . I'm not sure quite often when I get to work how long it will go on or what will happen. You explain what you want, but in the end you're not totally sure really how it will go. It's always fly-by-the-seat-of-your-pants. You're just throwing out a number of ideas.

Laura sometimes goes even further down the route towards children choosing their curriculum:

I'm in control but that doesn't mean I don't allow the children within these boundaries to make lots of decisions for themselves. That's what it is for me, that's what education is about. It's for the children to be making decisions. How wonderful to have a child who comes in wanting to write a story. 'Please can I do my maths today?' Lovely that they want to do things, that they've got ideas, that they have a need to write something.

These are just some of the more prominent differences among these teachers. It will be seen that creative teaching is not a style which can be defined in standard categories. It is, for example, neither child-centred nor didactic. In fact there are, paradoxically, more instances of didacticism in terms of transmission of factual knowledge within the classes where more control for the children is encouraged over the content of their curriculum, than in classes where there is a more teacher-centred curriculum. In the latter, more 'elicitation' is used, in which pupils use a trial-and-error method to arrive at the correct answer. In the more discursive engagements with children, the teacher makes statements and then some critical questions are debated.

COMMON CHARACTERISTICS

The teachers also exhibited a number of things in common, including independence, a humanistic approach, strong moral purpose, a concern for equity, teacher- as well as child-centredness, firm control, and strong emotional investment in teaching.

Independence

These teachers had minds of their own. They were not, for example, bound by ideological premises, for example of progressivism or child-centredness. Grace had a spelling programme as part of her project; Laura handed out grammar worksheets from time to time if she thought it appropriate; Theresa did basic number work on most days. All three of them engaged the pupils in sport. Grace took them ice skating and played rounders regularly, Laura taught her Year 2 pupils football and

Theresa arranged evening trips to an Arsenal game. Theirs was not simply a pragmatist philosophy, but one built on other educational principles related to a broad context of experiences.

Though independent, they were not 'laws unto themselves'. They had a strong collaborative spirit, and were often seen talking informally to other teachers about their practice. They discussed educational issues with them endlessly. They were strongly appreciative of other teachers and acknowledged their debt to them. They were innovators, were very quick to bring new techniques and experiences into their classrooms, and learnt quickly and readily from others. They worked very publicly at an institutional level, engaging in many hours of curriculum debate and planning. They generally ran and attended more courses than other teachers, and were often involved in further study. They were also the ones most likely to be interested in new initiatives.

A humanistic approach

The teachers were strongly resistant to the burgeoning bureaucracy that was threatening to submerge teaching as human engagement in the wake of the 1988 Education Reform Act (Campbell *et al.* 1991a). Theresa articulated her basic humanistic aim:

> teaching children to be people. You might use work to do it, you might use academic fact to do it, you might use information to do it but basically what you're doing is teaching somebody to be a person who can cope and who can be reasonable, rational, sociable. You get back to this hidden curriculum. That's what good teachers are teaching. They use a lot of vehicles to teach it. They may tart it up with something else, they may use a cosmetic, fancy academic tag for it, but what you're actually doing is teaching people to be people.

This aim conflicted with some recent developments:

> I doubt very much that a Conservative government would see me as one of their good teachers. Like when I send in the records, most people's are immaculate but mine aren't. And in terms of the number of things ticked on pieces of paper and so on, I'm particularly weak, but, then again, it's almost an unconscious political statement to be like that. It's not that I'm unable to do it. In fact, I'm very good at paperwork. I spent a hell of a lot of time in secondary schools doing nothing but paperwork, and my administration is very hot. But having made the conscious decision to come back to the chalk face, there are a number of factors which, I think, are more important than having a bulging folder or having all my targets ticked.

Laura also felt that where there was such a heavy emphasis on record keeping, 'You teach to the records and in a sense your teaching content is done so as to produce material for your records. I didn't do that actually last year, I just felt like working for the children. Making them the primary client.' Grace agreed: 'It takes time and if it was only that, but it isn't only that. We have other meetings to do with other aspects of the school. If we could just focus in and forget about all the other things, the recordings and everything else and just really put the emphasis on the quality of teaching.'

A political purpose

Teachers exhibit various different degrees and types of commitment: instrumental, professional, vocational (see Sikes *et al.* 1985). Our teachers had a strong moral and political investment in their work. They had a strong sense of values that they wished to convey through their teaching. Laura, for example, saw her commitment as political:

> I think what Paulo Freire said is absolutely right. It's a political decision for whom are you teaching. You have to make a decision and the decision you make is political and if you think that you are teaching because that's the best thing you can give to those children then that's the decision that you've made, and you have to make it because it's the right thing to do ... I'm very much for the sort of world that is not patriarchal or matriarchal. I want a world where we live in some sort of mutual respect, and I want it for my sons and my daughter and for me and for all the children.

Equity is strongly to the fore among their values, and they want to breed a questioning attitude among their pupils. Thus, though Grace described herself as a traditionalist in the field of sexism, she had joined girls in her class in challenging pornography, was developing a curriculum that encouraged her pupils to search for stereotypes and was keen to have a classroom where children questioned assumptions. She wanted her pupils

> Not accepting everything that they come across, questioning, and being able to pick up on certain things that don't quite make sense. Questioning what it says in that book and asking 'Why does it say that, Grace?', and to go and see another book. I want to encourage that. But it's hard work.

Theresa used history to face burning political questions that interested her. She recognized that children were not 'innocents' (King 1978), and could handle hard issues and abstract concepts, but felt the need for some mediation:

> You're reflecting on today by using the safety net of the past ... I wouldn't want to bring the Falklands War ... or the real war in the Middle East into my classroom, because I may in fact have to look

at bodies in the classroom. But I can bring in the concept of war through the Armada, and do it quite simply. I can bring all sorts of appalling things into my classroom quite safely. I can bring the concept of hanging, slaying and quartering in, and I can deal with that brutality because it's historical and it becomes a fairy story. I would no more think about tackling necklacing in Soweto in a classroom than fly through the air, but I can tackle far greater brutality by saying it belongs to the Tudors and Stuarts. So incredibly sensitive issues can actually be brought out in the open, and then when they get dodgy we can put [them aside]. This is what I have tried to do with the Tudors and Stuarts. By talking in this school about women's rights, a lot of people would think it was [inappropriate]. Many families here live in very conservative family structures but I can live with many feminist issues, I can be blatantly feminist and get away with it, which I do under the blanket of the Tudors. I can float out to those extremities as a point of triggering discussion, of getting other ideas out. But if I start to bring out issues today I've got a pile of crap in the middle of the floor and I can't put that away, and pupils will go home and say this and this, and people will get uptight about it.

This is not to say that hard realities were turned into fairy stories, or otherwise transformed into fiction through history; but rather that these devices were used as media through which the children could come to terms with those realities. Laura told of early stories concerning her family and the gender discrimination that existed in her mother's times. Her mother, though unqualified, taught special needs children, and was once quizzed by an inspector for being innovative. The inspector said,

'What are you doing?' and she said, 'They're practising their reading, and I use these different colours to help them', and he said, 'Oh no, they're not supposed to learn to read, they're ineducable.' And there was that attitude about it. You can't do it because they've already been defined. I can remember her feeling really upset about this, that she'd been told she was not doing her job properly.

Laura admired her mother for the way she trained herself, and became experienced in pedagogy, mainly through trial and error, and also for her understanding and commitment to the people with whom she worked. These personal experiences, in turn, affected Laura's perception of her role as a teacher. She was interested, for example, in influencing her curriculum in terms of gender:

I like doing things like cooking with them because it's a traditional female occupation which has been devalued, and I like to use it for science and revalue it because they just enjoy it so much. They love it, it's a nurturing skill. It's caring, it's hospitable, and it's cross-cultural in that it provides windows on to different cultures. It's chemistry in action loads of the time, more science than is actually going on in the National Curriculum.

Teacher-centred, as well as child-centred

The situation for these teachers is a dynamic one in which the teacher is clearly pivotal. Their classrooms were teacher-centred to the extent that they either orchestrated everything or they created atmospheres to ensure a particular form of learning or engagement (see Chapter 5). They all spent a considerable amount of their time in front of the class or on the carpet (or quiet corner) with them. They were not ghostlike figures drifting through the class just facilitating learning (Alexander 1992). Theresa tried to underplay her part in orchestrating involvement but it was obvious she played a large part in determining the climate of interest and enthusiasm in her classroom:

> Storytelling is very important. A lot of the excitement created is not necessarily me, but I give out some vocabulary and that vocabulary may trigger their excitement. What I do, like today's stuff [a lesson where the children drew close-up pictures of one part of an athlete in action for PE week] triggered all sorts of different excitements for different children, because immediately Richard got quite geed up about football because that happens to be his passion, and Pete got himself geed up about rugby because that's his passion. So in fact the excitement I created was very little. What I did was to actually press a few buttons that got them to create their excitement.

These teachers did facilitate learning but they also created learning through their purposive and direct teaching approaches.

Grace had what she described as a baptism of fire when she became deputy head of an infant school. She described herself as being unambitious but someone had pushed her into making this move and she immediately regretted it when she saw the teaching approach in most of the school. After a term a new acting head arrived and they discovered they had similar feelings about teaching. Partly because of the catchment area and partly because of the dominant teaching philosophy it was not an easy place to work:

> There were kids rolling on the carpet, there were kids shouting all the time. It was patently clear that they had no structure. I was in the open-plan area and the noise level was horrendous. I had children coming in from other classes, they were so bored they were coming in and wanting to do what my kids were doing. I used to go home and cry. I was as miserable as sin and I thought I cannot cope with this ... When the new acting head came, we instantly clicked. She

taught me so many management and teaching skills. She just had so many ideas, she just blossomed in the classroom, just watching her in action was an eye-opener, she had a vast experience, a bank of ideas because she was in her fifties. She was a pleasure to watch and she was exciting. She got the kids all looking and listening and up on their knees and full of enthusiasm . . . She was constantly bubbly, constantly exciting, constantly providing umpteen ideas and busy, busy, busy. It was all a busy, active, noisy, but very productive class, and yet some of her activities, some people would turn their noses up and say, 'that's very formal'. It was constantly busy and every child was covered in a day and she believed that every kid needed little and often. She was able to get kids reading faster . . . She made life easier for the other teachers by simple little techniques and very quickly within two years she had that school running smoothly, she had much happier kids and less harassed teachers.

The dichotomy between formal and informal classrooms has bred further distinctions between 'teacher centred' and 'child centred' to describe differing primary classrooms. These teachers show that the reality is far from these distinctions, with a mixing of approaches, a 'goodness of fit' (Alexander *et al.* 1992). These approaches also include similar attitudes to control.

Control

Control was basic to these teachers' practice, but it was a control tinctured with their other qualities: humanity, moral purpose and care for their children. Grace explained how she coped with her classes:

The effort went into the planning rather than the recording and the assessing and the ticking and the flicking and everything. My main job was to keep those kids busy and to keep them as happy as possible, to minimize the tension and the behavioural problems. But if anybody else came in and tried to take them, they couldn't handle the class, I mean they were a tough class. Cynthia [the head] was pleased. She used to bring people in and show them my class and whatever we were doing, and I felt I had achieved and succeeded as a teacher. I felt the kids had learnt. I kept the lid on it and I thought those kids were basically quite happy. If children aren't happy they're not going to learn. You had your odd fights and odd friction and I became quite skilful in dealing with this, [mainly through] humour. It was a lot of affection, teasing the life out of them and cracking the odd joke. If I told them off and shouted and screamed, all it did was cause a reaction. So it took every ounce of affection and ounce of humour to keep those kids basically happy . . . There was always lots for them to do. They didn't have the chance to be bored, but I didn't have the chance to sit.

Laura was not alarmed when she was told that she spent about a quarter of her time with her class on the carpet:

> Whenever it starts being a time when they're losing track of what we're talking about, then I know it's time to shift it. Other times they obviously need to talk and it takes longer. We don't have a set programme where I'm thinking 'I'll spend ten minutes at this and that', it rarely works out like that. Sometimes it does, and I give directions and orders for the day and then we go and get into it. But we come back to the carpet to find out how people are doing and let them present their work and then go back to it again.

Laura exemplifies a strategy used by all the teachers we encountered, that of being in front of the class for a considerable amount of the day. It will be shown that the time is spent on purposeful and productive activity, but it also shows the extent of control that these teachers had over the classroom situation. This was not, of course, the only method of classroom organization used, as we shall see.

Desire

> Desire is imbued with 'creative unpredictability' (Lasch 1990: 66) and 'flows of energy' (Deleuze and Guattari 1977: 26). The basis of creativity, change, commitment and engagement is to be found in desire ... In desire is to be found the creativity and spontaneity that connects teachers emotionally and sensually (in the literal sense of feeling) to their children, their colleagues and their work. Desire is at the heart of good teaching.
>
> (A. Hargreaves 1994: 12)

These teachers were passionate about their work in many of the conversations we had with them. They felt strongly about the subject matter of our discussions. They showed a variety of emotions and exhibited varying degrees of anger, depression, resignation, anxiety and hopefulness. These passions concerning their practice were reflected in their pedagogy. For example,

> Theresa started the afternoon session by encouraging the group to tell stories about that morning's sports day at the park. This was helped by Theresa's graphic storytelling using a wide vocabulary, humour and lots of metaphors. She defined and interpreted in a way that provided a rich picture of the morning's events. She then asked them to create a newspaper account of the morning's events, to be taken home that night and presented to parents. She always makes children's activities purposeful and active. She spoke of how she moved from tiredness to active involvement, and when asked what drove her,

she answered 'enthusiasm'. Not the enthusiasm of the individual teacher, but of the situation, the context of the children and teacher together which increased the adrenalin. She was swept along by 'the good times'.

(Field note)

Grace was asked what contributed to the children's success. She outlined overt emotional strategies, used to such an extent that they drained her emotional resources:

> Sometimes I tease them, or I'll say, 'caught you out on that you know', and 'no, you couldn't do that, you wouldn't be able to do that, you can't do those sums'. But Tanya can, and they want to prove that they can do it and that kind of gets them going, like David, when I said to David 'you can't do these, no, David they're too hard for you'. All of a sudden he wants to do them . . . I can only say it's the variety of tasks that are offered to them . . . it's gauging it so that they can all come away at the end of the day thinking 'well, I did that and I did that and I did that, Grace, I did all those things today. I feel good about it.' I try things that are practical like the measurement today. They loved it and they ended up measuring my head and going round measuring all the kids to see who had the biggest head, and they really enjoyed that. Junior made his book, although he wasn't sitting with everybody else, at least he made that little book and he wanted to read it to the class at the end of the day, which is not like Junior. He actually said 'Grace, can I read this to the rest of the class?' It shows that he really felt it was worth showing. But that takes a lot out of me, you're catering for this one and that one and this one and that one all the time.

These teachers, because of their moral commitment and the emotional drive they put into their teaching are among those most at risk of burnout (Woods 1990), as Theresa indicates:

> You just come in and do it and go, don't you? To me it still seems quite interesting that before not too long I will have spent 25 years in teaching and it just seems ludicrous that one's burning so hard and so bright after 25 years. After 25 years one should be honed and it should be skilled and effortless as if you were watching a kind of blacksmith after 25 years or you were watching a potter after 25 years. They wouldn't be putting such strain on their heart or such emotional strain into what's happening. It's almost like sulphur burning, isn't it? It's frightening and it's getting more difficult and we're giving more to children. I don't think the way that I teach is physically or emotionally the easiest way to do it. I don't think it is the most cost-effective way of doing it.

CONCLUSION

The teachers featuring in our research were a varied group in some respects, with some significantly differing approaches and experiences. But they do have a number of things in common. Strong moral and political values underpin their practice, and they feel passionately about their work. Their fully committed, all-embracing practice – moral, technical, political and emotional – is mentally and physically challenging. These teachers, despite – indeed ironically because of – their strengths, are particularly vulnerable to marginalization through creeping bureaucratization. This delimits the all-embracing practice, affects the quality of their teaching, and leads to heightened stress. We shall consider more of these problems, and how they were being tackled, in Chapter 3.

3

A NEW PROFESSIONAL DISCOURSE? ADJUSTING TO MANAGERIALISM

A MANAGERIALIST DISCOURSE

The last ten years have seen a concerted and determined attempt by central government to transform the school as a workplace and teachers as a workforce. Intensification has increased workloads, expanded bureaucracy, colonized teachers' time and space, reduced flexibility and separated the conceptualization of policy (made by others) from its execution (by teachers) (Apple 1986; A. Hargreaves 1994). The introduction of the market ideology into education has brought a new emphasis upon managerialism. Teachers' work is being more closely regulated, with a strong emphasis on accountability to the consumers – school managers, governors and parents. The 'social market' model of professional learning sees teachers as products of a training system closely geared to prespecified outcomes and the behaviours that lead to them (Aspland and Brown 1993). New divisions have opened up among practitioners between managers and teachers. Ball (1994: 64) observes that

> the reinscription of power relations in education attempted by the Education Reform Act offers the potential of a massive over-determination of the work of teaching. In this heterotopia of reform the relationships of teachers with their significant others are changed and confused; the teacher as person and professional is both scapegoat and victim. Professionality is replaced by accountability; collegiality by costing and surveillance.

Inglis (1989) argues that managerialism retains power by suppressing moral and political argument, and turns responsibility and accountability into functions of State surveillance. There is also a restructuring of teachers' skills in process, with de-skilling in some areas, though enskilling in others. Ball (1990: 98) forecast that 'teachers will have less responsibility for deciding what they do, where and how', though he also noted that 'grand intentions are not always realized in practice and may actually be contradicted'.

With these changes has come a shift away from the styles of teacher professionalism that have prevailed for much of the century – that of either 'licensed' or 'regulated autonomy' (Dale 1989) – towards a new form based on a market-driven technical-rationalist ideology (Hatcher 1994). Primary teachers have thus been faced with a new form of role conflict: between their identity as relatively autonomous, creative teachers and their new function as managers of a new curriculum system. The new role requires a considerable amount of administration relating to plans, assessment and record keeping. The introduction of limited devolved budgets also means teachers have to spend more time managing their school. Since primary schools typically have a small number of highly collaborative staff, this means that many teachers are involved in all kinds of decision taking in the school.

The changes have been framed within a new legitimizing discourse involving a whole new thesaurus of terms and everyday practices, and the key concepts of choice, accountability and quality. Maguire and Ball (1994: 11–12) argue, following Foucault, that

> a discourse is only ever partial, is only one stance among many variants. However, some bases for interpretation or definition become more dominant than others; power and knowledge are redistributed. Some voices, some modes of articulation and forms of association are rendered silent. Certain possibilities are offered and others are closed down, some ways of thinking are supported and empowered, others are inhibited. Actors are positioned and constructed differently within different discourses, different values and ends and purposes are operant within different discourses. The task then of the progressive educator is to reappropriate key discourses, to deconstruct dominant meanings and reassert more democratic, participatory and socially just meanings.

There are some studies that suggest this can be, and is, done. Ball and Bowe (1992: 101), for example, argue that the Education Reform Act in one respect is 'another micropolitical resource for teachers, LEAs and parents to interpret, re-interpret and apply to their particular contexts' (p. 100), and that 'it is in the micropolitical processes of the schools that we begin to see not only the limitations and possibilities state policy places on schools, but equally, the limits and possibilities practitioners place on the capacity of the state to reach into the daily lives of schools' (p. 101).

Fitz (1994: 60) comments that ' "implementation" is rendered as a

complex, creative, and important "moment" in the cycle, in which practitioners are conceptualized as meaningfully interpreting, rather than
simply executing, policy which has been "handed down".' Fitz points out
that the 1988 Education Reform Act is 'as much about restructuring institutions – defining new goals, delineating fields of operation and reconstit-
uting membership of the policy community – as it is about promulgating
substantive educational policies' (p. 60). Within this area of restructuring there appear to be a range of possible adaptations (Simkins *et al.*
1992; Woods 1995). Hatcher (1994: 49) observes that 'the restructuring
of teachers' skills, and the extent to which teachers are retaining some
control over conception as well as execution, is a matter for detailed empirical work.' He also feels that 'the struggle to create this new school culture takes place on the terrain of teachers' professionalism' (p. 55). It
is in that area that we concentrate in this chapter. We might expect our
teachers to be well to the fore in any such struggle.

We focus on the tension felt by teachers between their basic values, en-
capsulated in the role of 'creative teaching', and those of the new managerialist role. The substance of this tension can be summed up in terms of
'going with the flow' against 'getting done' (Apple 1986). 'Getting done'
is characteristic of bureaucratic systems, where an objectives-led approach,
with the emphasis on outcomes and monitoring, focuses attention on getting the prescribed task finished and records completed regardless of
what other opportunities for learning occur during its course. 'Going with
the flow' – a term that encapsulates our teachers' approach – puts the
emphasis on process, and involves intuition, spontaneity, 'tacit knowledge',
enthusiasm and fun. In speaking about the changes, teachers employ a
professional discourse which is both a way of expressing their concerns
and a way of handling them. It is a restatement of their values. In this way,
the events of the past few years have been an opportunity – for reexam-
ination, clearer exposition and evaluation of the practical application of
those values – as well as a crisis. We shall examine the main features and
characteristics of this discourse, together with the teachers' experience of
the new managerialism. Currently both approaches sit side by side in the
teachers' daily lives. There is a sense of struggle and conflict, of oppres-
sion and loss; but also of hope, resolution and creative adaptation as they
feel their way towards a new professional discourse within which they can
contextualize the changes ushered in by the 1988 Act.

Here we consider three prominent areas of conflict suggested by our
research, focusing on teaching approach, the use of time and accountability. In each case, we note the pressures, but also the progressive adaptations, as far as they go, through which the teachers seek to re-establish
their ownership and control of their own teaching. We conclude by examining the price paid for their endeavours – high levels of stress and guilt
– but noting their continuing resolve.

TEACHING APPROACH

The pressure for 'getting done'

Our teachers, like others reported elsewhere (for example, Campbell and Neill 1994; Pollard *et al.* 1994), were in favour of balance. They welcomed a National Curriculum in principle, but were concerned at the amount of content and the effects managing its implementation would have on their kind of teaching. Thea, for example, recognized the need for structure and progression, things that were not much in evidence before 1988, but felt things had got out of balance:

> There are certain things that you have to get done that these children have to cover during the course of their time with you. So that pressure has taken away a lot of what I consider to be our imaginative [role], the spontaneous side of teaching and lighting a spark in children. You still do it. The National Curriculum has many good things to it as well, but you can't organize your topic in quite the same way as you could before because you have to bear in mind all the attainment targets.

Ends had come to predominate over processes. Peter, a deputy head, thought the National Curriculum

> certainly has cut down opportunities for taking an idea and developing it. I have more now in mind where I want to end up in terms of ends, and I'm not sure that's altogether healthy. It's certainly not healthy to say we can go anywhere – you've got to set boundaries and a sense of what is worth pursuing – but much more these days I get the feeling that if a child offers something that doesn't actually fit into my National Curriculum target, then I'm more likely to say, 'yes, you've got a good idea there, it's worth pursuing but we haven't actually got the time now, let's see what other people are offering.' He's not slapped down, but the opportunity of something going in a slightly different direction from what one envisaged originally is shut down a little more often. I think it's a pity too because occasionally it's a child's idea or contribution that may have been stimulated by thought processes that might have led to something that might have lasted a quarter of a term, half a term, a couple of weeks.

Reaffirmation of 'going with the flow'

Even in the above, it is possible to detect signs of a professional discourse attempting to make sense of, and to contest, the new order. There is a recognition of the need for balance, a reflective analysis of what is involved, and a reasoned resistance. Above all, however, there is a reaffirmation of the principles in which they believe, and the kind of practice which those principles imply, that can be described as 'going with the flow'.

'Going with the flow' is important to our teachers for four main reasons. Firstly, spontaneity affects the atmosphere of the classroom and the enthusiasm of child and teacher alike. As Laura said,

> If there's something there that children are really, really enthusiastically interested in, it would be so silly to ignore it. Because the motivation's there. It's already made, the eagerness, the drive to look at something, to find out about something. It's already there. You don't have to stimulate it, you haven't got to set it out. It's a gift . . . It's the energy and the curiosity, the desire to know is satisfying so they feel good about it, that they've asked the question and answered it and it stems from their need to know, and it's like saying 'Yes, what you're thinking is important, let's explore it'. It's not saying 'no, not now dear, we've got to do this, much more important, could you pay attention please' and I start complaining because they're not listening.

Winsome describes just such a moment that really did flow:

> We had this massive block of ice which was about 18 inches by 24 inches that somebody brought in off a drainpipe. There was a bit of drainpipe in the middle of it. It didn't melt for two days, so we weighed it over the days, we floated it, we had a wire cutting through it on weights, different kinds of wire all stretched across, some plastic-coated, some different metals to see which metal cut quickest. We did friction experiments, sliding it around on different surfaces, all sorts of things. We flooded the headteacher's office because it dripped through the ceiling. Then other kids brought in lots of icicles and we did lots of poetry and stuff about the ice and icicles. And that was fine. In those days you felt that was OK to spend two or three days doing science, or if you got into a project like a particular book, or a particular painter and children are involved in a painting, it didn't worry you if they spent two days doing painting and you would find the stuff that they had produced at the end of it was really something. Whereas now I would rush them along to finish it in the afternoon. So I think you sacrifice some of the quality which you had for quantity.

Eddie expresses many of the teachers' responses about the feelings they have for their work:

> I think a lot of it depended upon the teacher's enthusiasm. It was difficult not to be enthusiastic. It was actually great to go into work. It's a long time since I felt high about kids' work, but I remember the feeling you get in your chest of almost wanting to cry because something has really, really got to you about a child being successful. It's a fantastic feeling and it's not as if you as a teacher are on an ego trip, because it's not what you've done, it's what the child has done and that more than keeps you going. It nourishes you.

Eddie, however, feels that 'this intuitive, teachable moment type thing is in danger of being something apart and I think if that were to happen I would find teaching so appalling.'

Secondly, 'going with the flow' enhances the learning process for *all* children. Particular pupils need more help and assistance. Winsome argues that a 'one best way' system is not effective for these children. She thinks, 'We need to ease up on them a bit and look at where they are and try to give them what's appropriate for where they are.' Theresa supports this approach in generating what she calls her 'hidden curriculum' – teaching people to be people:

> Because basically the hidden curriculum has got to do with not being too organized . . . It's about letting go of that and letting things sort of drift. It's kind of knowing how much to let it slip. So I would have to think very much about the real quantities and the real actualities of what I do there. I have let a lot of situations ride and roll – like good referees in football matches.

Thirdly, 'going with the flow' encourages pupil control. Marilyn explained:

> I was thinking about this week's close observation art and how I got children to say how they did it, how they achieved it, to the rest of the class. They're taking part in the instruction really. They're taking a role in teaching themselves, they've learnt something and they can pass it on to the rest. There's a huge value for them to know that they have that value and that you've got children who are talented in different areas. It does motivate them because they will look at that and they will go away and try it or they will try another angle on it.

Fourthly, 'going with the flow' enables teachers to concentrate on the learning, rather than on record keeping and monitoring. Terrie commented: 'In times gone by you could probably be more open to just taking off at a tangent if the children were interested. Somebody brings something from home and you could develop so much around that.' Thea also rued the threatened loss of 'those spontaneous topics that you used to be able to have, say if children brought something in . . . You could give it a certain amount of time . . . the children spurring you on, rather than you saying, "Well, this is the way it is".'

There is an acknowledgement of threat here, and almost nostalgia for lost times. Things have certainly changed. But the educational reasons for 'going with the flow', the gains to the child, the thrill and excitement of learning at such moments stay with them. Their convictions remain. They stay devoted to the principles. In a way, the Education Reform Act might be regarded as a natural experiment, in which their values and practice have been put to the test. They have had to search their consciences, not only in the light of political rhetoric, but also of academic research, where Alexander (1992), for example, has raised questions about ostensibly child-centred practice, which, in his research, 'paid rather more attention to teachers and classrooms than to children's learning' (p. 143). There is ample testimony here to their reasons for, at times, 'going with the flow', and they are couched largely in terms of pupils' learning. Their actual practice will be studied in subsequent chapters.

The tension between 'going with the flow' and 'getting done' is not a new one for primary teachers. They are constantly juggling a great number of demands upon both their time and expertise. However, the balance between these two demands seems to have shifted radically, and particularly with the inroads being made on teachers' time and space. 'Going with the flow' requires some flexible time and a considerable degree of mental space: time to be with children, to teach, to potter, to discuss with colleagues, to read, to listen; space to reflect, to think, and to have ideas. However, both time and space have been squeezed in the inexorable concern to 'get things done'.

THE USE OF TIME

Pressure on time

As A. Hargreaves (1994: 95) points out, time greatly structures teachers' work, and is, in turn, structured by it. Time is a different element in 'going with the flow' than in 'getting done'. In the former, it is more flexible, multidimensional, people-orientated; teachers and pupils *make* time, and above all, have a sense of ownership and control of it. In the latter, it is more objective, task-orientated, compartmentalized, unidimensional, rationed in segments, controlled by others (see Woods 1993: 147–8 for further discussion). A. Hargreaves (1994) claims that teachers' time, which they previously owned and controlled, is becoming colonized by others. How much time teachers have to do their work is an issue, but even more important is the use to which it is put and who controls it.

Teachers employed a number of strategies in coping with the attempted colonization. We noted the following:

Distancing

There were considerable pressures on teachers' time, in terms of the sheer amount of work. Theresa, expressing the difference between technicians and professionals, argued that the National Curriculum could provide an easy way out for some teachers; but she distances herself from this adaptation, reaffirming her own professional identity, and incurring in consequence a vastly increased workload:

It's because you've got a set parcel, haven't you? If somebody tells you what to do it's much easier than if you've got to think for yourself. Someone who has not got decisions, somebody who has not got choices to make, that's fine. The lazy teacher can get through a certain amount just as long as she satisfies the National Curriculum. The good teacher spends an awful lot of time on development, tension from the National Curriculum is undermining. They do three times as much work, fine, OK. If you teach the National Curriculum you don't have to worry that much. You've cut your work in half. If you're a good teacher you're teaching the National Curriculum *and* what you were teaching before.

The perception of alternatives

Apart from the sheer load, there was a question of quality. As with Cockburn (1994: 377), our teachers found it difficult to achieve 'high quality teacher time working with their pupils'. Campbell (1993b: 220) has shown that nearly ten per cent of teachers' time is 'evaporated time', taken up by activities such as moving pupils around and supervision. However, the main threat to quality, in the teachers' opinion, was the intrusion of bureaucracy upon teaching. Laura expresses it here in describing how she has to fill in detailed records to obtain some government funding for new books for the school. The colonization is clear, but it is prefaced by the comment that there has to be a better way. The hard-edged intrusion upon Laura's time is thus morally undermined:

> It makes you think there's got to be another way of being alive, and of working ... where actually you know what you're doing (for example, filling in records) is wrong. Where I'm spending today and tomorrow filling in these records it's not for the children's benefit ... it's an accurate record but it doesn't enhance the children's learning ... They want this record, we've got to do another record for our National Curriculum records, make sure children have been delivered, have achieved, and then of course, we need to do another record altogether that mentions that we actually taught them to read, because of course, they could achieve all sorts of statements of attainment and still not be able to read, which is another problem ... I was up on Thursday night till three o'clock in the morning doing these and I'm not even doing as many as some other teachers ... I don't think anybody would mind so much, spending all this time if you really felt that the children's learning was being enhanced ... Now we're actually thinking there's so much work involved, is it worth this amount of money? I mean what has been wonderful is that we had £600 to spend on books in this classroom. However, I'm doing more than £600's worth of work to get it because of the extra hours of paperwork I'm doing.

The use of other resources

Marilyn told of how meetings out of school hours 'impinge on your actual teaching'. The night before, for example, she had had a departmental meeting followed by a governors' meeting. She arrived home 'brain dead', unable to plan her teaching for the next day, or to advise her daughter on her homework. The week before, she had had meetings every night, and felt in consequence that she had not achieved much during the day: 'You need to sit down and think where individual children are and what they haven't finished. If somebody makes a comment, you've got to follow that through the next day and if you know they haven't understood what you've said, you've got to plan some more work for them in that area.' However, at times, salvation was at hand:

> On Monday I did a piece of work on tenths and I realized that there was a group of children who hadn't got a clue about tenths of something. I wanted to sit and plan some work for them. I was late on Monday, I was late on Tuesday, there were finance committee meetings and something else. Fortunately, I had the students (teacher training), and I said to them, 'Can you do some work on tenths?' One went away and planned it, showed it to me, and I said 'Great! Go and do that with that group of four', which was brilliant. I only needed the time to talk to the student rather than needing time to sit down and organize it, get together the stuff I needed. She did all that. But if she hadn't been around for me to say that, I'd have been thinking all week, 'I must find the time to plan that one activity for an individual group of children that hadn't been planned at the weekend'. It's squeezed out by all that meeting stuff.

Reaffirmation of pupil ownership of time

Teachers rehearsed the need for pupils to have time and space in which to work, as Marilyn does here:

> Knowing that they can choose to discuss work with me and being able to have time and space to discuss is important for them to know where they are in their work, and I also think it's important to give them time to experiment. With a lot of the tasks that are set, writing for instance, if I'd been heavy about them sitting silently on their own it wouldn't have worked so well. Children need to have that space to talk to someone and very often you'd look at them and think what are they talking about? Nine times out of ten if you went over and sneaked up behind them to listen they'd be talking about writing. The book reviews done in groups was giving them a kind of space as well. It certainly was a lot of time to give to one piece of work because that's very time consuming because they all want to have their say. Certainly you could rush through a piece of work and put it to one side and start something else and you actually get a lot more stuff on paper. All that time taken over one piece of work was incredibly valuable because it moved them on in their next piece of

work. Next time they did a book review they remembered what went on in that interchange. What somebody had said, 'about your organization, couldn't you just . . . ?', 'What about the characters?'

Contrastive rhetoric

The term 'contrastive rhetoric' was coined by A. Hargreaves (1984) to describe a strategy deployed by senior managers in a school to secure collective decisions for one option by ridiculing others. In this way, the managers 'translate institutional power into interactional power' (p. 15), though it does require the acquiescence of the collective. Our teachers used contrastive rhetoric, not so much to ridicule or belittle – things were much too serious for that – but to delineate and expose.

The teachers were conscious of the need to keep records and to monitor pupil development. They were enthusiastic about innovations that improved their pedagogy or their understanding of individual pupil needs. Most of the schools, for example, used the Primary Language Record, which entailed keeping detailed records of each child's language development. However, some were finding it necessary to organize their teaching materials to satisfy new, less educationally sound demands. Laura, for example, observed others teaching through the assessment worksheet and felt this narrowed the learning situation. There 'wasn't time to do anything else':

> The reality is the teacher does a worksheet with all sorts of little drawings on it with various things which are balanced or not balanced in different ways and asks the children to check these, and if they do it all right they will be considered to have gained that concept. So the worksheet acts as the teaching implement, the assessment and the record.

In one conversation with Laura we looked at a transcript of a chat between the researcher and a pupil in Laura's class concerning some of her work. Laura found the extract fascinating and commented:

> That tells you a lot about the way Natalie was thinking. Tells you a tremendous amount about her. It tells you about her relationship with other children, her feelings of ownership of her work and that she's able to give it away when she chooses, and develop new ideas. There's loads and loads of things in there that are really important about Natalie that levelling the National Curriculum doesn't add to. An orange highlighter on an attainment target doesn't tell you anything, does it, about Natalie's skills? The real records are the words she says.

The qualitative record, according to Laura, is the more appropriate record, for it appears to contain more information and the whole person at the same time.

Grace pointed to the loss in reflective planning time:

In the past I would stay after school, potter around, get my resources
ready, think about what I'm going to do, have everything ready, much
more leisurely, and next day be well prepared and it was all nice. But
the balance is wrong, I'm doing records. This weekend I did about
seven hours work that had nothing to do with the way I was going to
teach on Monday morning. I was doing minutes for language meeting, minutes for staff meeting, summary of the half-term reports. I
had to do a reference for a teacher who left. I had to do my reading
samples and write them up, my reports, about seven hours, and none
of this was my classroom work. Monday was given three seconds
thought.

Laura explained how the energy teachers relied on to generate a creative climate was being diverted to more bureaucratic approaches:

I feel the informal network was stronger, because there's only so much
energy attached to it. Energy is limited, you just get tired after a while
and because the network was stronger [in personal terms] and because
there was more time to talk, you felt more relaxed about things in
the past and so there was more time, not only to support members of
staff who did need it, but to notice members of staff who needed it,
and I think this is occasionally being misheard. I mean the support
that was offered in the past was much more in the nature of a sort
of informal, friendly, helping hand. Whereas now one is more likely
to fill in a form and write down what the problem is and it's sometimes quite difficult for somebody to articulate what their problem is
because in a sense, if you can articulate what the problem is you've
solved it. So it takes quite a lot of talking around to find out what the
problem even is.

REDEFINING ACCOUNTABILITY

Accountability is a major feature of the new professional managerialism,
and was something that had to be confronted by our teachers. Following
Foucault (1977), Poulson (1994: 3) notes a change in the meaning of the
term, being seen 'less as a moral obligation to clients and colleagues,
either individually or collectively, than as an aspect of the disciplinary
technology by which the work of teachers and schools is surveyed and
controlled'. In the market ideology that currently prevails, education is
a commodity sought by consumers, whom the producers, consequently,
have to satisfy. Accountability is then used 'to establish a discursive
consensus which constructs teachers and schools as being in need of

external regulation' (see also Epstein 1993). Poulson (1994: 11) noticed that, in the secondary schools of her research, her examples, 'which indicate how accountability is used, understood, interpreted and re-interpreted, seem to indicate that although a specific term such as accountability may recur in accounts given by different actors in relation to particular issues, meanings shift according to those specific contexts.'

Our teachers sought to construct their own meanings of the term and its implications within their own preferred contexts. The sheer pressures generated led Grace to refer to it as 'heavy-duty accountability'. At once, this designates it as unwarranted on workload and rational grounds:

> If you think of the last five years since we've had the National Curriculum, we've had to get used to it because there're millions of attainment targets, and we've had to learn how to teach science. There was so much to kind of adapt to. Then they changed it, so then we had to change what we were doing in the class. We had to look at the way we were planning. We had to be able to include everything in a balanced way in the planning, because it was all new and the planning was all new, it was real heavy-duty stuff. Then, when they [inspectors] came in we had to be able to say why we were doing this planning, why we were doing this . . . and then they wanted to see the records and the evidence, so we had to be able to produce the samples, umpteen million samples. For five years it's been that heavy-duty way that has never really changed because we're always reviewing and evaluating and changing it. Refining it, and refining it, and even now after five years we still are haggling over the way we should collect the evidence. How we should select, how we should mark. You know even now we still haven't got it right.

It was 'heavy', secondly, because teachers did feel under a kind of sinister surveillance. Terrie voiced her fears:

> I worry about the fact that somebody's going to march in and say 'Oh, what's this covering in the National Curriculum?' If you've got the gift of the gab, you can immediately call to mind the connection and defend yourself. I suppose I feel all the time that people might come and say 'Oh yes, but you haven't done this, where's all your technology, where's your science or your history, or your something', and I think it constrains you from being brave enough to actually just do what you want to do.

Grace commented:

> You know all the time that you're having to assess, all the time you're having to prove and give evidence of the work that you're doing and the children are learning and being appraised and people coming

into your room. To me it's really like checking up on you. I hate going into other people's rooms [appraising]. I loathe it, that's the part of my job I hate the most. I feel worse than the person whose class I'm in. I just wish that that could be left and we could just get on with teaching without pressures, without demands and bring the fun back in and the relaxed way we have. I'm sure it would do us better, we'd feel better, we'd feel less stressed and therefore it would affect your teaching in a more positive way. I don't mind the National Curriculum, but the rest . . .

It is a short move from here to attacking the credentials of those to whom they were accounting. It seemed to the teachers that these people lacked the knowledge and expertise to warrant their authority. This increased the sense of burden, but also aided the transformation of the exercise to one whereby they could consign this key element in the managerialist discourse to the ridiculous. As Grace said:

And you know what gets me? . . . We have inspectors coming in and they say, 'it's not sufficient, your sampling isn't sufficient here, or your records aren't varied enough in your reading,' or 'There's too much of the same thing, or your writing doesn't . . .' You need the best of what the children do, rather than samples each time, and you feel we still haven't got it right. The inspectors have criticized everything. But why haven't they told us what's right? They've been into every frigging school in the country and they still can't tell us. 'We have visited 6,000 bloody schools, we've seen *this* way of sampling, *this* way of sampling, *this* way of assessing, *this* way of recording', and they cannot tell us why we are spending five years going round, trying to get it right. They have learnt so much about different schools, why can't they pick out all the best and say 'well actually in this school we're doing this. It doesn't overload the teachers, it's very effective and it's a great way of assessing kids. In that school they're doing this. That's another way you can combine the two and you'd have a brilliant record-keeping system.' No, we haven't had one bloody word of advice . . . It's like a crystal maze, you're going round all the time and not getting anywhere. You're not getting out of this turmoil . . . this whole mesh of record keeping and mesh of paper and mesh of admin, and mesh of time-consuming wasteless, wasteless, valueless paperwork. I said to our local inspector the other day, I said, 'I'm so angry talking about records', I thought, 'I can't take this any more.'

This extract conveys the intensity of Grace's feelings concerning the innovations, though she, like most teachers, is by no means an opponent of many of the reforms. She spends a considerable amount of time on records. She is instrumental in co-ordinating and attending a vast range of meetings in her school and she uses the National Curriculum as the cornerstone of her curriculum planning. The root of her anger lies in the perceived uselessness of so many of these procedures. She asked one inspector, to no avail:

> 'Why do we have to collect these bloody samples? Just go and look in their books for God's sake. Why are we photocopying out of the books to stick in the bloody folders so that when you come in you've got to look there and you've got to look there and you've got to look over there. The books are evidence, what more do you need? We collect all this stuff, we put it in folders and none of us look at it.' . . . I said to him, 'when we do these observations I jot it down in rough because I cannot do it in best copy'. I'm not clear-thinking enough to do that, so I kind of scribble down all the notes, and then I think, right, I must fill that in, on the record sheet and maybe ten days later I fill it in and I do it all and I think, yes, what this kid needs for further development is, say for example, it's electricity. What this kid needs for further development might be a bit more work on circuits, more complicated circuits, but by that time, by the time I've done that we've moved on to light, so who gives a shit what's written in that little box.

Grace keeps her folders amongst her shoes because she wants to 'trample them to death'.

> Why am I spending Saturdays doing records and writing them out, why? The only thing I think is worthwhile is the reading and writing records. I don't mind doing them, but all the other stuff, taking out samples of this and that, no way, and I'd say most teachers feel exactly the same . . . because heavy-duty accountability is destructive. We all come in on Monday and we're as ratty as hell because we're too tired. It takes me longer to eat my vitamins and my pills than it does my breakfast.

The inability, in her terms, of the inspector to answer her question satisfactorily, plus her observation (backed up by other teachers, Laura specifically), that nobody actually checks on the records they make, further undermines the educational legitimacy of this form of accountability.

Finally, there is the question of to whom teachers are accountable. The new order puts the emphasis on parents as the main consumers of the new education. This is acceptable up to a point, but again, there is a taste of the 'heavy duty' about it. Terrie expressed a typical attitude, reaffirming the teachers' view of professionalism:

> Parents know a lot about education but I like the kind of attitude of listening to what you do and commenting and adding things like that,

but I think because the debate has been shifted out so much to the public I can't bear the idea that I'm being utterly accountable to parents. I'm sure you are to a certain extent and I respect a lot of people who have advocated that but again the feeling that people are standing in the playground and talking about teaching methods I should adopt that come from on high is a bit much. I mean doctors and solicitors don't get told how to do their job by their patients and clients.

By designating the process as 'heavy duty', identifying and reacting to the implications of surveillance, attacking the credentials of the monitors, denying the usefulness of the exercise, and reaffirming their own professionalism, the teachers were reconstructing the notion of accountability in their own discourse. They are under pressure, but fighting to retain the moral ground.

EMOTIONAL CONFUSION

The result is, despite mental clarity, considerable emotional confusion. Teaching is not a well-paid job in terms of salary. Hence the importance of intrinsic rewards (Lortie 1975; Nias 1989), and the necessity of feeling right (Riseborough 1981). Many teachers have not felt right for some time. For many, the fun has gone out of teaching (see Campbell *et al.* 1991a). For example, Sandra commented,

I don't think there is as much [fun]. It's still there, but it's artificial. Everything seems much more artificial than it used to be. As a staff we don't really discuss the deep-seated issues as far as education is concerned, but a lot of my time is spent chivvying along, calming people down, trying to make things sound a bit more positive, just generally humouring people.

Laura stayed in teaching because

I actually enjoy it, but I think sometimes the frustration level is such – the paperwork and the record keeping – I wonder whether I should move on to something else . . . The frustrating thing is, having done it, you don't even feel that slight glow of pleasure when like you've done an essay . . . you think 'Oh wow! I've done it at last!', even if it's tortured you. You know it's been a waste of time . . .

The fact that these teachers were so emotionally involved with their work and felt so passionately about it meant that they were highly vulnerable. They felt these tensions deeply, and, though imaginative and innovative people, did not always see a way forward. This is a classic recipe for the generation of guilt and the onset of stress. Hargreaves and Tucker (1991: 495) note that teaching is attended by 'guilt traps', many of them deriving from the fact that

> in the context of teaching, doing or failing to do what is right is more than a matter of personal moral choice. It also involves the context of caring and the extent to which that context enables or restricts the exercise of such choice. Teachers may, for instance, be prevented from doing what is right as they wish by insoluble dilemmas or impossible constraints.

Grace argued that the process of record keeping was eroding confidence:

> All it's doing is slowly eroding the confidence. I used to feel a much happier, comfortable confident teacher and now I think I've become uptight. Now I feel I've got to get this done, I've got to get that done, don't talk to me, go away, you know, and I hate it. Yet I put in more effort, I'm working harder than I've ever done before. I'm working harder and yet spending a lot more hours doing school work but not doing class work.

Nadine illustrated how the tension between her conception of teaching and 'heavy-duty accountability' produced guilt feelings:

> I will always decide how I teach, I know they don't dictate that and I'll always do it the way that I think is best for them but I don't like the guilt feelings. I don't like the thought that if I, say, spent a whole term on doing something that we all really enjoyed and it's not in the National Curriculum, at the end of the year I have no box to tick and people will say I'm not accountable. I haven't covered subjects that I'm supposed to have done, I haven't planned a topic that has covered enough.

Nadine looked forward to seeing her children in the morning and 'having a chat . . . Listening to their stories about things which I don't always have enough time to actually listen to what they want to tell me.' She felt that to some extent you can still 'go with the flow', but 'you feel guilty about doing it because you feel that you're not doing the other things that you should be doing.' If you concentrate on 'getting done', however, you feel that 'it's eroding what children want to do, what they enjoy, how they learn through their own experiences.' Nadine had got to the heart of this tension by indicating that whichever way teachers went, they would feel guilty. Terrie also could no longer 'go with the flow'

without feeling guilty and feeling 'Oh, I haven't managed to do this or I haven't done this attainment target level', whatever it is that you're supposed to be doing. I feel that I can't really do that now. Although I feel I should, so I'm really torn, I feel I should be working for the children. To a certain extent I do, but I don't feel I have an opportunity to really go for it which I'd like to do.

The sense of guilt for Nadine derived from a profound feeling of moral and social responsibility:

A part of it is feeling that you can never do enough for them. You haven't got enough time to see everyone and do maths with everyone. Also it's to do with the National Curriculum in that you feel that to give them the best chance, you have to do as much of the National Curriculum as possible, whereas the other half of you says that you know that what you are doing is better for educational reasons. But you feel you've got to cover it all otherwise they're not going to get the best chance because that's how they're going to be tested in the future and you want them to have the best chance although you know it's not the best way. It's all about the aims and purposes of schooling – the government's imposition of the product model. It's undervaluing exactly what teachers do. It's almost saying to us, 'you haven't been doing it right, you're not doing it right. This is what you should be doing.' What teachers do is just say we are doing it right, we can do it right, we're going to do what you're asking us to do in our way, but it won't stop us feeling guilty about not doing enough. All the time there's a mismatch between what you want and what you think is best and what they're imposing. It's like you're being pulled in different directions.

This is a classic stress syndrome (Woods 1990). That most of these teachers do remain in the system and manage the guilt traps in some form or another is a credit to their powers of survival. However, it is achieved at some cost. Theresa talked evocatively about her teaching experience and how managerialism was affecting her:

Most teachers have got an inbuilt sense of survival, haven't they? And as far as I'm concerned, my philosophy is, let's get something on the rails that gives me the most time to breathe . . . We've been around long enough, we've seen it all, haven't we? What do you say about it any more? . . . Every year we end up giving more to children and having to give more to children and every year the job gets wider and more diffused. There is inevitably going to be an end to the elasticity of what teachers can give. And I would've thought we're coming very near to most teachers being inadequate to what is being asked academically, intellectually, socially, emotionally, physically, financially, in terms of comfort, very, very close to the end. I think I can run longer, harder and better than most people I've come across and I'm finding it hard work. I think I can do that because I've had more experience of it and I've been given opportunities to see a lot of tricks of the trade . . . And if I'm finding it hard going, Christ! some people must be finding it crucifying!

Laura, on the other hand, had managed to fight off feelings of guilt about doing something different to the National Curriculum, seeing this as an exclamation of her humanity:

There's got to be humanity and part of the humanity of it [teaching] is that sometimes I've had enough, but I still feel OK about saying to the children, 'I'm sorry I can't'. It's not often I do it but I do feel if I do it, it's OK. I don't feel guilt about this. I don't feel that this is wrong, I just feel that we operate at such a high level and so intensely most of the time that it's OK that sometimes you just tick over for the day and you finish things up and you relax and have a chat with the children and quite often something else really good takes place and it's not to do with the National Curriculum or anything like that, it's to do with all sorts of other things.

This may seem to imply that Laura only went 'with the flow' at set times outside National Curriculum periods of teaching, but that is not so, as we shall see later. Again her comments have to be seen in the context of the professional discourse. Nevertheless, she was giving an example of how her philosophies and integrity are bound up in her work (see Nias 1989).

There is anger, frustration, stress and guilt here in teacher reactions. There is also a sense of deprivation. But running through the comments is a sustained commitment, resolve and sense of moral purpose: 'I actually enjoy it', 'I will always decide how I teach', Nadine's 'looking forward to having a chat with the children', Theresa's 'survival', Laura's insistence on 'humanity' . . . At times, they are run a bit ragged by the new demands, but this thread of positive emotional reactions buttresses the mental aspects of the new professional discourse – at least for the moment. The danger is, perhaps, that the discourse becomes privatized or localized, and, in consequence, distilled or dissipated. Peter recognizes that here:

I have to keep on telling myself there's no way I'm going to cover it all, but I can't say that too often in public and yet in a way, I think, that is what teachers need. They need to know that there are a lot of us who really, honestly think we can't get it all in, but it has become a hidden something or other not to say so. People don't say it too often except in jest or in a flippant way or sometimes angrily, but we don't sit down and discuss this together consciously.

A NEW PROFESSIONAL DISCOURSE

We would argue that there is a more positive outcome contained within the discussions in this chapter than simply feelings of exhaustion, frustration, rage and stress, though those are real enough. What is being generated here is a new professional discourse to combat that of professional managerialism. Foucault (in Weedon 1987: 108) defines discourses as 'ways of constituting knowledge, together with the social practices, forms of subjectivity and power relations which inhere in such knowledge and the relations between them'. They are based in institutions and realized in practice, but 'these institutional locations are themselves sites of contest, and the dominant discourses governing the organization and practices of social institutions are under constant challenge' (p. 109). Professional managerialism may still be the 'dominant discourse', but there is sufficient discursive space to allow resistance, and 'resistance to the dominant at the level of the individual subject is the first stage in the production of alternative forms of knowledge' (p. 110). This is a 'complex and unstable process whereby discourse can be both an instrument and an effect of power, but also a hindrance, a stumbling block, a point of resistance and a starting point for an opposing strategy' (Foucault 1981: 101).

The new professional discourse may be embryonic at this stage, but since the Education Reform Act of 1988, there has been an easing of the government's position (see Dearing 1994) and we might expect a concomitant strengthening of the alternative professionalism (see Hatcher 1994). Its main features as manifested in our teachers are, firstly, reaffirmation of the principles that underpin teachers' practice. Secondly, there is resistance to those elements in the changes that run counter to those principles. There is a reasoned opposition, again at the level of values, on both pragmatic and moral grounds (Bridges 1994). Some of the changes do not work, like, for example, much of the bureaucracy and the overloaded curriculum. But the government are wrong anyway in trying to run education like a business. A feature of the resistance is taking the attack to the enemy, as in, for example, Grace's assault on the inspectorate, or Wendy's on excluding the teacher:

> It [the National Curriculum] does not include the teacher in the equation, it only wants to quantify, there's nothing on quality, there's nothing on what makes a quality teacher. Everyone knows what makes a quality teacher really, but it's never written down. It is things like their rapport with the kids, their own life experience, their interest in what they're teaching. The idea that you can standardize and have uniform teaching without taking into account how the teacher feels, the mere fact of overloading the teacher with all this bureaucracy is going to have a negative effect upon their teaching, and I just think it's all just too prescriptive. You've got to do electricity with fourth

years, design a model in this, put in Tudors and Stuarts this term. It's like trying to impose secondary teaching on primary teachers. You're a class teacher and people just don't work like that. You don't have half an hour of maths, half an hour of language and half an hour of technology . . . I think it's the fault of the system, that the teacher is not put in the equation. The teachers' feelings, what motivates them and their energy, and their enthusiasm is crucial to what happens in the classroom.

There is, thirdly, no blanket condemnation, however, of the changes. They give a balanced verdict, one that acknowledges the educational bene-fits in the National Curriculum. They are aware of the dangers of return-ing to a 'free-for-all', and admit to some of their own previous inadequacies. Fourthly, a number of strategies are employed to counter and neutralize the effects of managerialism, such as distancing, perceiving alternatives, and the use of contrastive rhetoric. Fifthly, there is a transformation of some of the main tenets of professional managerialism, namely choice, quality and accountability. Choice becomes professional choice, espe-cially with regard to teaching methods. Quality is a matter of framework, some records, balance and adjustment, emotional attachment, and moral worth. Accountability under professional managerialism becomes, in the new discourse, 'heavy duty', a shorthand description for time consuming, stressful, and useless activity. They prefer an accountability located within professional values, best judged by their peers. Sixthly, the emotional character of some of the responses indicates both their passionate com-mitment to their work, and the recognition of the part played by the emotions in the teaching and learning process. This is in stark contrast to the technical-rationalism of parts of the National Curriculum and par-ticularly of its assessment, which seems guided by behaviourist principles (Pollard 1991). This emotional engagement is certainly out of tune with professional managerialism.

Finally, there is an articulation of solutions. In amongst the pressures, there were signs of confidence, optimism and opportunities. For example, Terrie said:

I have to reach a happy medium, I'm sort of wavering between either doing very prescribed National Curriculum going down one route, or else taking off into something that the individual finds fascinating, that I want to do . . . I suppose as you go on a bit, you feel more con-fident about doing this and doing that. I just feel that you have to be able to defend yourself in the face of it. Although it doesn't happen, no parent comes in to say . . . but somehow you feel that they might.

Nadine noted that, intrinsically, it was possible to do adventurous topics *and* meet the requirements of the National Curriculum:

The stuff we did on giants doesn't fit anywhere into anything but it does fit into bits of everything. A lot of design and technology came out of it, a lot of writing, a lot of language work . . . I had to do a topic on electricity . . . I did it in my way and the best way I could for them, but it wouldn't have been something that I'd have chosen the very first year of Year 2 if I hadn't had to. And I worked it all around my own way by using a story about who'll be the sun – I just worked it all my own way.

Nadine thus found her own way round the necessity of having to do topics that she did not think appropriate – a significant feature amongst these teachers in general. Theresa commented:

If I decide that I'm going to make it to head then I will provide an environment where eight to twelve people could teach like that. If I ever became a head then I would put most of my energies into making sure that those people were free of the constraints that could stop them working. And I would spend my time making sure that they were facilitated and being able to do some of the exciting things that we have lost. If I decide not to be a head I shall go on in a class-room hoping to be a good teacher and just having a deaf ear when people ask you to do things. And becoming even more and more selective as to what I do and what I don't do.

Laura found a way of resisting increasing bureaucratization by a new kind of collaboration. She engaged in team teaching with a close colleague and found this liberating

from two different angles, coming out at it different ways. When two people do things and you spread the load tremendously the record keeping has got two brains working on it and hopefully that minimizes it and we get it done more quickly, more effectively. But I think the most important thing about working as a team with another person is the support that you get and that you're not feeling very isolated and vulnerable. I do think teachers are feeling very vulnerable at the moment about whether they've done things right and having another adult working closely is tremendously supportive. You know, you really do feel supported and you don't feel that you're constantly doing everything wrong where you're not actually quite meeting the criteria.

Andrea proposed a solution that indeed became law as a result of teacher pressure:

I am a very impulsive person and if I think of something going along in the car on the way to or from school I feel that I am very limited by the fact that I can't say, 'Well, I am going to scrap what I have done

and I am going to do this today.' That is the worst thing about it . . .
I wouldn't want it to go to the sort of laid-back feeling where you
thought you could do anything, and nobody would bother, and there
wasn't any assessment or record keeping because that would be wrong.
But it would be nice to perhaps have a day a week when you could
just decide what you wanted to do and have a fun day. We do have
our art days when we blitz.

Shortly after this, Dearing (1994) announced his plans for rationalizing
the National Curriculum, making it more manageable, and giving schools
the equivalent of one day to pursue their own curriculum – what Laura
referred to as Dearing's fifth day of 'civilization'. However in advocating
this resolution, Andrea seemed to have accepted the dominating nature
of bureaucratic processes.

There need not, of course, be a clear-cut solution for a discussion to be
helpful. As Laura astutely observed in an earlier quote, 'If you can articulate what the problem is, you've solved it.' Though the teachers bemoan
the pressures on their time, the heavy accent on 'getting done' and new
forms of accountability, it could be argued that their formulation of the
problems constituted a step forward. They are with the 'significant minority' of Pollard *et al.*'s (1994) teachers who felt that 'a new professionalism
involving creative ways of working with individual children was possible,
provided they had the confidence to shape the imposed changes to more
professionally accepted ends' (p. 99). There is a kind of political activism
here, not one characterized by attempts to engage directly in trying to
change policy, but as articulated in the course of everyday interaction. Its
importance lies in this exercise of power, and in the production of a truth
and knowledge within which their professional selves can work. As Ball
(1994: 22) notes, 'We do not speak a discourse, it speaks us. *We are* the
subjectivities, the voices, the knowledge, the power relations that a discourse constructs and allows. We do not 'know' what we say, we 'are' what
we say and do . . . This is a system of practices . . . and a set of values and
ethics.' A discourse is as much about actions as words. Others have found
vast differences between what teachers say and do, depending on context
(for example, Keddie 1971). How far, then, was their alternative discourse
evident in our teachers' practice? Aspects of this discourse make up the
remainder of the book.

4

THE EMOTIONAL SIDE OF TEACHING AND LEARNING

The emotions figured prominently in our teachers' work. They were passionate about their own beliefs, as we have seen; they cared for their children; and their teaching had a high emotional content. This is not at all unusual in primary schools, and has been seen by some as having strong gender connotations. Steedman (1988), for example, argues that elementary education in the nineteenth century, under the influence of Froebel and Pestalozzi, grew out of ideas about mothering in the middle-class home. 'Good mothering' implied 'attention, identification, empathy with the child' (p. 122), but what the mother did naturally needed to be 'made conscious' in the teacher. At the centre was the 'idea of growth as a natural unfolding, a kind of emotional logic of development' (p. 123). It required the provision for the child of opportunities, flexibility and spontaneity. One consequence of this was that middle-class teachers found it difficult to empathize with working-class children, though the 'caring, domestic homeliness of the peasant mother who loves her children' (Burgess and Carter 1992: 350) came to be added. Walkerdine and Lucey (1989) speak of a 'sensitivity discourse'; and Burgess and Carter (1992) of a 'Mumsy discourse', which they claim to be the predominant moral technology (Foucault 1975) operating in primary teaching. Being 'Mumsy' involves many of the features of child-centred education, such as 'bringing out the best in each child'; shaping personalities; seeing children as people rather than learners; socially approved feminine virtues like caring, nurturance, warmth, understanding, comforting; strategies of discipline operating through caring; regarding the class as a family. But it also involves sacrifice – the traditional sacrifice of the mother for her children (Grumet 1988); the continual treadmill of never-ending work; 'overconscientiousness' (Campbell *et al.* 1991b); and the acceptance of blame and the generation of guilt when achievement falls short of aspiration (A. Hargreaves 1994).

Walkerdine (1986) argues that the prevailing discourse operates to preserve the norm and existing power relations in a patriarchal society. She claims, for example, that women teachers are forced to absorb the violence and aggression of male children through caring, while supporting the passive, caring role of girls, and thus helping prepare them for future work in the caring professions. The child-centred ideology is thus a trap: 'Women teachers became caught, trapped, inside a concept of nurturance which held them responsible for the freeing of each little individual, and therefore for the management of an idealist dream, an impossible fiction' (p. 55).

'Caring', by this argument, is not adopted as a free choice, but is part of the reproduction of sexual divisions in the family and the labour market. Its force derives from it not being just an activity, but an essential constituent of the gender identity. Women are bound to the ideology by strong feelings. Caring is an act of love (Graham 1991; Thomas 1993).

Interestingly, the government has had an ambivalent attitude towards this discourse. On the one hand the discourse came in for strident criticism in the moral panic that attended the assault on primary pedagogy in 1992 (Woods and Wenham 1995) on the lines of there being 'too much caring, and not enough teaching' in our primary schools. Inasmuch as a number of these principles were enshrined in the Plowden Report, they came in for blanket condemnation under that banner. Some academics have supported this argument. Alexander (1992), for example, argued that primary teachers were in the grip of a child-centred ideology which constrained their practice. Simon (1988) regretted the lack of a science of teaching, and the concentration on children's differences rather than what they all have in common. He argued, too, with Alexander, that there was an urgent need to prioritize the cognitive. At the same time, the professional and economic implications of a 'Mumsy discourse' were not lost on a government seeking economies and more power over educationists. In 1993, a consultative document on the training of primary teachers proposed, among other things, a one-year course for non-graduates to teach 5- to 7-year-olds. This was the so-called 'Mums' Army', an idea promoted by the Secretary of State of the day with the clear assumption that mothering skills were all that were needed in order to teach children in the early years. The plan faced strong opposition from teachers, who saw it as an attack on their professional status.

We recognize the force of this critique, both from a gender and from a learning theory perspective, but we also note an alternative argument, well put by Noddings (1992). She believes that 'the main aim of education should be a moral one, that of nurturing the growth of competent, caring, loving and lovable persons' (p. vii). She uses images of the family, urges teachers to see children as their own, and as unique human beings. As for the gender argument, she acknowledges that

> women's traditional experience is closely related to the moral approach described in ethics of care. Women, more often than men, have been charged with the direct care of young children, the ill, and the aged. They have been expected to maintain a pleasing environment, to look after the needs of others, and to mediate disputes in ordinary social situations. If we regard this experience as inseparable from oppression, then . . . what I am describing is merely 'slave mentality'. But if we analyze the experience, we find considerable autonomy, love, choice, and consummate skill in the traditional female role. We may evaluate the experience as essential in developing fully human beings.
>
> (p. 24)

Noddings is aware of the fear among feminists that promoting an ethic of care may aggravate the exploitation of women. But this is not a sound reason for removing it from the curriculum, though versions that include an emphasis on the menial skills of caregiving, and that differentiate between boys and girls, ministering to gender distinctions, should be avoided. 'The new education I envisage', says Noddings, 'puts a high valuation on the traditional occupations of women.' These are the kind of values that need to pervade society.

This view of teaching as a moral craft involving firstly the shaping of the generations of the future (Tom 1984, 1988) or person making (Brehony 1992) is emphasized again by Elbaz (1992). Elbaz's work with teacher-parents has led her to describe teachers' concern for children as being the moral nature of teaching. She is concerned that talk of caring and relationships risks placing in question the professionalization of teachers (Hargreaves and Tucker 1991). Elbaz (1992), drawing on the work of Ruddick (1989), compares teaching to mothering. The latter used to be thought not to require 'knowledge' since it was seen as producing nothing of material value, and hence was not real work. Ruddick argues, therefore, that we have to find new ways of conceiving of maternal work. Listening to mothers talking about their experiences helps. Similarly, Elbaz (1992) argues, we need new ways of conceiving of teachers' work. One way is by giving voice to teachers' knowledge which is 'not merely one of recognizing and describing this knowledge, but calls for the invention of a language and conceptual categories which will support new ways of talking about teachers' work and thought' (Elbaz 1992: 423). This invariably brings out the moral dimension in teaching, showing it to be much more than a technical exercise: 'we should be aware that to focus on teaching as a moral enterprise rather than an exercise of technical skill is ultimately to challenge the technocratic and patriarchal discourse of western culture' (Elbaz 1992: 422).

How these values can co-exist in teaching with a high level of political awareness is well illustrated by Sikes (Packwood and Sikes 1994), a teacher-trainer, who found, on becoming a mother, her views of pupils undergoing a profound transformation:

> I entered classrooms and found that in some bizarre way other people's children had become my child too. I now cared about the children in a way that I would once not have thought possible. I felt for them, I enjoyed their company, I enjoyed their questions and their attention, I even, in a certain sort of way, loved them.
>
> (pp. 10–11)

As a mother, she became more patient and tolerant of her own students, and acquired new perspectives on the world. She suggests that motherhood and specifically mother-teachers have not been studied academically because they are 'relatively powerless' and fall within the category of the 'silenced' (p. 13). But clearly, in her experience, motherhood vastly enhances the teacher's disposition, capacity and understanding, and it would help, in her opinion, if some of these 'silent' teachers had the opportunity to speak. We might all learn something.

We give voice to teachers in this chapter to show the professional basis of their views on the part played by the emotions in their teaching. We argue that our teachers, not all of whom were women or mothers, used emotional connections with a view to extending, developing, encouraging, and liberating the child and increasing choices.

PERSON MAKING

Basic to these teachers' outlook is the child as a person. The National Curriculum, by contrast, treats the child as a student. One of the main responses to the National Curriculum from our teachers was that it left out many aspects of primary teachers' responsibilities. In their attention to 'person making' (Brehony 1992), they were concerned with the personal, social, emotional and intellectual development of children, Theresa's 'teaching people to be people'.

However, in attempting to define the knowledge necessary to achieve her ends Theresa is more mystical:

> The secret of teaching children is to do with a kind of freemasonry of communication ... Handing them the secret things, handing them the Holy Grail ... I can't really get any closer to it than coping really. It's a very hidden curriculum. It's difficult to explain. Because that's the curriculum you carry with you all through your life, and the National Curriculum doesn't encompass that.

This chapter is an attempt to get beneath that mysticism and focus on the characteristics of that communication. The subjectivity involved in the triad of relationships between teacher, pupil and the knowledge to be learnt (Bonnett 1991) is central.

Marilyn here describes the sort of social skills she sees as important in life, as well as how they relate to a learning context:

> Communicating with other people, knowing boundaries between different sorts of groups of people, because they're there and we've got to know how to approach people, how to react to people when they talk to you. Mutual respect has got to be an important part of school because if they don't have it I don't think they can learn in the way that I want them to learn. I want their learning to be sociable. If you've got an expectation of active learning, they're going to have to do it together. They're going to have to work together and to be able to relate to other people. It also means being able to relate to anyone in society really and that's all part of the work. It's so interwoven really. This is the whole life skills thing. You can't be involved with the whole child by ignoring social skills because no matter how academically inclined or disinclined they are, they really need those social skills. Basically, I want them to make it in this world.

Wendy sums up this holistic approach:

> I think it's an essential part. It's why I teach in primary not in secondary, and I did go to train for secondary. For me, the reason I enjoy primary is that you're teaching the whole person . . . their creativity as people and their social and interactive skills. That appeals to me. I like dealing with the whole child, and I don't think that leads at all to a wishy-washy, airy-fairy, woolly approach to education. I really think the structure and discipline of the mind is as important as social skills and emotional well-being, but I think they all go together, and I'd like to see them more integrated . . . I don't see how one can really separate education from the whole child.

And for Marilyn, there is no question about what her role is, or how many times she has to forgive her pupils:

> You do it for as long as it takes. For me, as long as I have that relationship with a child I'll keep working at it. I would have to keep finding other ways of working at it, changing strategies perhaps. I like them, you know, I want them to make it in this world. It's my job. I will maintain this argument no matter who says otherwise. My job is not just sticking facts in their heads. I take the responsibilities far greater than that. I'm not going to say it's a minor part of my work, it certainly isn't, but far greater is that they come out at the end of it, reasonably well-educated, responsible, socially acceptable human beings.

How does this concern for the whole person translate into practice? There are two contexts: the personal and the social.

The personal context

Teachers consider it important that the child be valued as a person.

Respecting the individual means that you care for difference. Wendy describes her relationship with a refugee child: 'With Tanzy, it was finding a structure. She's very structured, she's had loss in her life – people dying in the family, she's had help with things like that. We found a way through, whereby we could actually structure her work, through writing a diary, because free writing was very threatening.'

On a visit to the National Gallery with her class, Theresa had a very difficult time with one boy who had a tantrum at the gallery and was abusive, fought against restraint, and was difficult all the way home on the tube. He was suspended for the following day after consultation with his mother, and the following field note describes how Theresa talked to the class the next day about the incident: 'He did a lot of damage to himself but we all know and respect how much progress he has made. We think he has worked very hard in this last term. I am not going to throw him out, I'm going to see him tomorrow. If he does come back, as far as we're concerned, it's over.' She mentioned later that she was helping him to direct his attention to the task in hand and this was part of the progress he was now making in the classroom.

Erica indicated that her aims are to bring out the best in each individual:

> I am very interested that they become confident and competent in their writing and their maths. Or as competent at each thing as they are able to be and still feel like a worthwhile person. I explain that not everybody is going to be a Mantovani or whatever, but the quality of our life is how well we do things each day. Not only the winning, those days when we are the most successful in the whole world. Quality of life is the daily business and pleasure in that I have just done a small piece the best that I can.

These teachers are very supportive of their children, as Carla (Year 6), one of Wendy's children, attests, 'She listens to people and their problems. She gets excited when someone with a bad attitude problem like Henry comes on very well. When he's on report or something she comes along and supports him. She does the same with minority ethnic children who speak English as a second language, giving them books to read to, and they learn a new thing every day.'

Esther is sure that we must not miss the moment to enhance a child's self-esteem: 'Always when children bring something in we should attend to it, we must use that moment or it will be lost, we must take it up and value them, being aware and just knowing when they're struggling, just being aware.'

The social context

The social context is also crucial to person making. Theresa sees the relationship between the 'social hidden curriculum' and academic learning as a 'chicken-and-egg job':

> This is a super, able class. They're probably the most competent class in the school and are coming from a very negative base because they've had such bad experiences. This is a chicken-and-egg job. I'm not so sure whether I can push those children any further on academically until we've actually solved the problem of the social hidden curriculum, so the sort of work you're pushing out has very much got to do with the social environment of that class . . . Those are the important factors, actually rubbing along with them . . . and most of them are going to have to rub alongside somebody else for a lifetime, so it's quite important to coexist with people.

Handling the tension between working with individuals and the class is described as a 'subtle art' by Wendy:

> It's definitely them getting to know you and also getting to know them and the more you know them – as individuals – is how we get them to really function as a group. I find the class works well and is disciplined, when they're happy . . . And I feel that if I am really dealing with their feelings as individuals, this affects the whole group situation. It's so complex, really – there's a sense of a kind of a standard of discipline, but also acknowledging them as individuals, which is quite contradictory in a way. I find it's a very subtle art . . . For me being a class teacher at primary school is so much about a group dynamic. That's something in the National Curriculum which doesn't even get a mention, yet anyone who's taught in a class knows that. It's to do with interaction between children, between them and your interaction with them, individually and as a group. I've got two different personae really. I've got my interaction with all of the children on a one-to-one and then I've got a completely different persona of me as the teacher of a group of 25. I just feel children can't concentrate on their work if they are really upset by somebody else. For a lot of the children the thing that's uppermost in their minds is their emotional state, particularly in inner-city schools where they come from very difficult backgrounds. Unless they can feel secure and happy in the classroom there's no way they're going to make progress with their work, no matter how bright they are. Not just for their emotional well-being, but for their academic and intellectual development it is necessary to have that stability.

The National Curriculum is of no help with respect to consideration of the child as a person, being more concerned with child as a student. This, then, sets up a profound dilemma for our teachers. How do they resolve it? We suggest this is mainly done through emotional connections, given the recognition that children are emotional people. How is this done, and how does it affect the child as a student?

EMOTIONAL CONNECTIONS

Children as emotional people

Teachers consciously attend to children's feelings in relation to learning situations and recognize emotional reactions as signals to be interpreted. Erica is convinced that to ignore the development of the emotions is to affect children's future development:

> If you try and deal only with the children's minds then you will get into a mess because that's not who we are. We have aspirations, we have feelings and I will look and sometimes I see a mess because some child you can see is emotionally distressed and teachers are under pressure because really for that kind of quality we have too many children. But we pay for it later in life. The whole nation pays for this – people not being able to relate well together, work together. If you have no self-esteem then people have to rely on other strategies to feel important.

Enhancing the individual involves, for Erica, separating the possibility of task difficulty from worth as a human being:

> I will watch particularly what is the child's attitude to learning if every time I put something in front of that child the child goes into a panic. I will deal with that because the child is not going to progress if the blocking issue is panic. Then, she or he has been made afraid of learning. She may be worried about being punished or even being looked at, but I get to the bottom of it. It is very important separating the child's abilities from who the child is as a person, because that is a great block to learning. If, because the child has failed at his task, and that is the measure of this child's worth as a human being, then that goes on and is reinforced and reinforced and that is going to block them. Then the child will be presented with something and will be fearful. Take away fear from learning and also understand what it is. That would unblock that child and she would become much more receptive.

A 'non-fault syndrome' was observed in these teachers' attitudes to their children. They would often find explanations for a child's behaviour which separated the worth of the child from the specific situation. Excuses were found for being late, 'unhappiness creatures' were conjured up to explain bad moods, tiredness to explain inactivity. These factors were portrayed as features of life which could be adjusted and manipulated by the particular child or by others. A young child may feel that they have little control over many factors in their lives to do with institutionalized schooling, such as having to be on time, swings in classroom atmosphere generated by the teacher, and not being able to write quickly. It seemed to these teachers that this lack of control should not become a defining characteristic of that particular child. By using this 'non-fault syndrome' it was then possible for the child to blame the symbolic or actual cause and discussions then went on with the teachers about how to overcome these constraints and hurdles. This process not only avoided children thinking badly of themselves as people but enabled them to take more control of the particular situation.

'Unblocking' is done by Wendy in a more formal way. She has a weekly therapy session where children share problems:

> When starting to work with the class, I said once a week we're having what I call the 'therapy time', where they bring up issues with other children in the class and for them to become more aware, the effect they're having on other people. One does it in all sorts of different ways. That's quite a formal way. I've done sessions on, like being teased – everyone works with a partner and says a time when they've been teased and how they felt. Their partner feeds back another time where they've said when they've teased somebody and what that felt like and why they did it. There was a general awareness of, talking about, feelings. It's interesting the ones who can't do it are the ones who get caught in the act of doing a lot of teasing in actual reality. So I use formal sessions like that, or times when I talk about feeling, sadness, happiness. Some of that work I put under the umbrella of RE, religious education, tuning in to where they are, at the moment.

Teachers' awareness of individuals as emotional people seems to relate closely to Bonnett's concept of 'authenticity': 'thinking is not simply a matter of having acquired an extensive set of public concepts, it involves one's attitudes to the content of what one has learnt and the quality of personal significance that one's learning holds – i.e. the authentic value that one places upon it' (Bonnett 1991: 281). He argues that the myriad ways – learning, thinking, understanding, perceiving, feeling, intuiting – in which consciousness is in contact with the world, relate to those basic concerns which make us the individuals we are: 'Genuine thinking, then, cannot be abstracted from the individual's sense of their own situation – their life – and requires that we are free to explore our concerns and are encouraged to do so' (p. 281).

Many of the child's concerns, therefore, are seen as being located in the emotions. Teachers see the building of relationships in which they connect with the children on an emotional level as an essential requisite for learning and development.

Building relationships

Erica feels that a warm, personal relationship is important because children will feel that they can take risks, and not be rejected as people:

I feel that children as human beings – their holistic development, their relationships with me and with each other – is for me, the first and most crucial thing because their attitude to learning and their own development will be affected by it. If they don't trust any adults or are unable to relate to each other when you sit them down to work together, the whole way that they are treated will show in the atmosphere. You know what kind of citizens you are helping to encourage to develop. So that is very crucial to me and very crucial to really what you can achieve, educationally, in the standard of the reading, the writing, all of it. How they are able to work, how inventive they are able to be. Whether it's going really against the grain of growth or with it, limiting or expanding.

We gain some insight into the nature of these teacher–pupil relationships through Marilyn's account of how she felt about her sixth-years leaving her primary school. She illustrates the extent of the bonding between teacher and class:

A couple of days after the end of term, I really, really missed them. I think we got so involved with each other with the end of term performance, and then there was all the leaving activities which some of them got emotional about... [I was] much more involved with them than I have been with younger children. They were a much bigger part of my life because of all this intense discussion we were having all the time. I really enjoyed the conversations with them.

Marilyn contrasted the secondary school model, where they 'don't have someone with that overall view... don't have the contact', and where 'a lot of human connection is lost'. The subject specialism in the National Curriculum brings that model closer to primary schools, but Marilyn feels that the depth of human contact should take priority – 'the cross-curriculum link is so important'. She feels her views are validated by the experiences of her own children at secondary school, where they 'achieved good grades, good course work, good homework for a couple of years, and then levelled out and lost interest'.

Mike, a retired college of education teacher, worked voluntarily in Marilyn's Year 6 class and he greatly admired her approach.

One of the reasons is that she builds it [relationship] up well over time. She's always got time, she's got time for John. John in actual fact dotes on her, depends on her and doesn't play up so much. He still does because he just can't help himself sometimes but she's skilled at knowing when to leave him to sit under that table for half an hour to an hour, where one or the other of us might have gone after him. She's very, very good at bringing them back, offering the lifeline, very quickly after confrontation. She's not a dominant person. She is quietly, quietly controlled, there's no argument about it, the way they settle down most of the time. It's her care and concern for kids, that gets across to people.

Is this not a sign of the 'Mumsy discourse'? Marilyn, on the contrary, points to some of the details that made this a positive factor in their work:

There was security for them at a time of great personal and emotional change. They were moving on, and in some ways all that coping with growing up for a lot of them. How they dealt with each other, how they coped with all the disagreements or jealousy, etc., but there was this security as well, they knew that this group was all right, they were OK even if they had arguments, even if they disagreed it could be sorted out.

. . . you get to know them and you understand little things like facial expressions, if they're not catching on to something. Look at their faces and you know they don't know what I'm talking about . . . So you can then build on that to find ways around things. You can have that kind of conversation which is on a personal emotional level but because you can have that you can also then have that about work. You can use that same way of talking to them about the work they're doing, so again you can draw out of them what they've already learnt, what they need to learn next, what they haven't learnt . . . They know that I'll be firm with them, I'll really give them a dressing down and hopefully, most of them, most of the time will take that on board but, they also know that next time you want to discuss work or the next time they've got a problem it will be OK.

When Junior (Year 3) was asked how he felt about Grace telling him off, he smiled and said she looked a little serious but she didn't sound angry. Mostly these teachers developed behaviour that really neither looked nor sounded angry, as some children describe later (see p. 81).

Nathan is aware not only of the effective value of the affective, but also of the danger in children becoming dependent on him. He uses judgement, therefore, to encourage his Year 2 children to turn to each other:

One of the big plusses about teaching this age range is the affection, and that's a good thing that it can be channelled into very effective [learning] – but it is a letting go, asking them to rely on themselves or turn to one another first, or to use something that they don't naturally want to do. They like the reliability and daily contact of knowing that they've got their stable person as their classroom teacher and I'm forcing them away from that.

Thea develops intimate relations by taking an interest in their preoccupations and by encouraging the children to write letters to her to which she replies:

I do make an effort to build up a relationship with the children as individuals as well as a group, and I'm part of that group. Not to the extreme where I am their pal, but where they feel more comfortable and secure in the fact that we're all working together. The younger they are the more they are going to think, this is the teacher and you do what she says, so I try to know little things about them, get into their interests, show them that I am interested in them. A lot of them are into this wrestling thing, so I'll ask them, about certain wrestlers and they look as if to say 'how come you know'? I get them to write me a letter every week, rather than do a diary, for my language work. When I was away recently they had a supply teacher and the day I came back nearly every letter was about the supply teacher who'd come in, who was so horrendous to them. They wrote 'He threw our work in the bin, and he was shouting at us, are teachers allowed to do that?' It's not that I let them get away with anything. I know you need to shout sometimes but I think it works better the other way.

Marilyn believes in the concept of 'freedom within boundaries'. There is an element of pupil power here, but not a free-for-all, totally child-centred power; rather one within parameters the teacher sets as a guide to the children's learning:

They do have choices about what goes on, but they know at the end of the day that I have set the boundaries and they more or less stay within them. Every now and then they try to change the boundaries or move them around, and they probably like the fact that there is an opportunity to negotiate certain things. They know that if there's something that isn't particularly inspiring they can approach me and say something about it. I suppose these particular children feel quite safe with me. They know me from way back.

Thus, emotional connections are established to develop the individual as person and in the group. How does this assist in developing the child as a student?

Learning as an emotional experience

Berger and Luckmann (1967) argue that the child passes through two phases of socialization: primary and secondary: 'Primary socialisation is an induction into society through the subjectivity of others and internalisation in this general sense is the basis first, for an understanding of one's fellow man and second, for the apprehension of the world as a meaningful and social reality' (p. 150). Berger and Luckmann claim that this primary socialization takes place under circumstances that are highly charged emotionally. They suggest that 'there is good reason to believe that without such emotional attachment to the significant others the learning process would be difficult if not impossible' (p. 151). The significant others in this case are the parents or those close to the child during this phase.

Secondary socialization involves the 'internalisation of . . . institution based "sub-worlds" . . . the acquisition of role-specific knowledge . . . role-specific vocabularies . . . and tacit understandings' (p. 158). This clashes with primary socialization. In order, therefore, to iron out inconsistencies between primary and institutional realities, secondary socialization presupposes conceptual procedures to integrate different bodies of knowledge. Learning, instead of being subject mainly to biological limitations, comes to be established in terms of intrinsic properties of knowledge to be acquired.

While primary socialization cannot take place without an emotionally charged identification of the child with his significant others, most secondary socialization can dispense with this kind of identification and proceed effectively with only the amount of mutual identification that enters into any communication between human beings. Put crudely, it is necessary to love one's mother, but not one's teacher (p. 161).

Later realities are seen as 'artificial' in comparison to the earlier 'natural' ones, so teachers try to 'bring home' the content

> by making them vivid (that is making them seem as alive as the 'home world' of the child), relevant (that is linking them to the relevant structures already present in the 'home world'), and interesting (that is, inducing the attentiveness of the child to detach itself from its 'natural' objects to these more 'artificial' ones.
>
> (p. 163)

Primary schools may be seen as a bridging experience between primary socialization and secondary socialization, though recent developments have sought to reduce the difference between primary and secondary education. For the moment, however, and certainly for the teachers in our study, the emotions are a major feature in learning situations. One aspect of how this is done is by establishing a common bond of humanity to bridge the gap between primary and secondary socialization.

Common bonds of humanity

Eve is certain that the 'common bond of humanity' (Berlak and Berlak 1981) reflected through her feelings makes a direct connection with the children in the context of a particular topic. This would appear to be a central feature of 'going with the flow' – its ability to capitalize on positive emotions:

> A lot of it is to do with the children needing to bond with you or they don't care whether they work or not . . . I went to Pompeii last year and I was telling them about that and they all asked me about volcanoes. What I would love to have done was to move on and talk about volcanoes and how they work because I think they are all fascinated by that . . . But I am trying not to because I know I have got to do 'Invaders and Settlers'. I have to do 'Romans invading England'. We shouldn't really be talking about Pompeii, I should be talking about 'invasion', the reason for invasion. So that's frustrating because I feel like I could get a lot more, I could go off in a different direction, but I know that I have got to stay on track of the invasion, and reasons for invasion. Even though I am steering it that way I wish I could go off at a tangent.

Winsome describes her relationships with the children in terms of 'fun':

> Looking back, I can see that there's a lot of interaction between me and the children. So much of what we did was me and then we sort of responded to each other and it worked. I will always remember having good relationships with my classes. I look back on it and although we were often pretty worn out we had a lot of fun, we did lots of things, particularly teaching and living in London. You know London was an oyster, we just went everywhere. We had lots and lots of educational visits, lots and lots of people coming in, visitors, parents, we really used the resources of the community.

The identification of self in the educational process is seen as a central factor in curriculum reform. Hargreaves (1992: 255–6) argues that 'the way teachers teach is grounded in the kinds of people they have become. To change the teacher is to change the person the teacher is.' Teachers are social learners, and the common experiences they have with children are grounded in their shared emotions. Nicola's common bond of feelings are again centred around enthusiasm;

> Enthusiasms rub off on kids. I don't very often go into a class and do things I'm not interested in because I know that I don't do it well. But if I am interested in a particular subject or area and I go in and do it, I find that the children actually pick that up in a way. They actually get enthusiastic as well . . . I just know it's a feeling. The thing we've done most recently is an example. We did a load of movement and I brought in some Greek music and taught a group of them a Greek dance that they then did in assembly and I was really enthusiastic about that (a) because I love Greek dancing and (b) because I

actually just love to see kids working like this and they were really happy doing it. They were saying 'Oh no, don't do that movement', and 'Let's put a clap in there and that might make it look better'. They were really getting into it and I was enthusiastic about it. That seemed to keep them on the ball about it and it went on for weeks and they did it extremely well. I'm not Greek but I've got lots of Greek connections. I go every year and I lived there for a while.

This common bond is not only related to emotional high points. Theresa stopped the classroom activity one afternoon and talked to the whole class about an incident involving some animosity between some children. From a field note, we see how she used her own family as an illustration to show how tensions rise and how they deal with them:

She tells her children that she is always prepared to listen to indi-viduals and is referring to some children who have fallen out with each other in the class. She uses her own experiences to make con-nections with the children through common feelings of distress, anger and anxiety. She describes her home where they have a house rule that nobody is allowed to go to bed without talking to someone. She describes graphically, and with some considerable intensity how the problem is always three times bigger the next morning if this rule is not followed. 'It's like a worm inside you that exaggerates the situ-ation and a mess is created.' She then asks the children involved to discuss the matter and they are encouraged to give their views and they discuss feelings and solutions. She treats it as a serious issue.

So, establishing common bonds of humanity is one means by which teachers establish purposeful teacher–pupil relationships. How, then, is the dilemma between relating to the child as a person and the child as a student resolved? One way is through what Eddie calls 'teachable moments'.

Teachable moments

Eddie describes 'teachable moments' in personal and professional terms involving spontaneity and enthusiasm, as illustrated in this example where the children had discovered a toad on their way to school:

Their concern about the toad was really touching and I think that was something that really needed to be spoken about and addressed. The amount that they found out about that toad was good in so far as it meant something to them because of their interest in it. They had initiated it by bringing it in. It wasn't teacher-directed and I think the amount that they learnt, or what they learnt was very, very valid. They found out the differences between frogs and toads . . . They found out that he rapidly got dehydrated, poor thing. He was quite sick actually so he couldn't be left in the water. They found out that in order to survive he needs to breathe air but he needs to be kept wet and all that sort of thing. They were really motivated. We had one of the biggest thugs in the class alongside some quite sensitive girls. They co-operated. They handled the thing far too much and we talked about handling it and the warmth of the hands and all that sort of thing. At the end of the day we decided we couldn't keep it here overnight and they actually took it over to Camden Street to the nature park that is there. They actually climbed over the fence and put it by the pond. They didn't want to do that. They wanted to keep it, but they made decisions and they decided that was best for it.

In the following instance Wendy uses emotional connections to good effect with a boy who had learning difficulties:

It's a question of knowing your children. One boy in my class has got severe learning problems, no sequencing at all in his writing. He found a cat and took this cat home and cared for it. It was injured and he bandaged its paw, and in writing about this it was the first time he ever wrote sequentially and I knew it was a turning point. It was significant, a sort of marker of his development and it's only if you really know the child and know where he's coming from, on the emotional level, that you know you can link in.

Her involvement was not just in reacting to him as an emotional being and unblocking constraints or removing fears, but by being willing and flexible enough to adapt the learning situation to that child's emotional interests.

Nathan's science topic on homes had an emotional connection. The children compared Bangladeshi and English homes, reflecting the ethnic composition of the class:

I grabbed somebody from the language and learning centre and the science advisory teacher and said, 'Come and work with me and Nadine' – a parallel class teacher. We were both working on the science course and I set this up because we were doing a lot of work that looked in a real solid way at life in Bangladesh. We were looking at the built environment, homes and houses. We looked in a very real way and used the children's knowledge and memories and experiences when we talked about what happens at home – cooking, washing and sleeping.

Winsome's work with infants used a similar approach:

These days I work more in the infants and I feel the same sense of panic because the time for the nurturing is pressurized. You constantly feel that there are all these various topics and pieces of knowledge that you have to get across, whereas previously it was more about socializing children, and covering basic literacy and numeracy within whatever sort of context seemed to fit for that particular group. I have seen infant teachers do a whole term's topic on something like teddy bears, or birthdays and they have been very successful, the children have done plenty of writing and illustration and analysing information and reading connected stories and so on.

This form of 'coming home' attempts to mirror the earlier features of primary socialization.

The emotions as 'common knowledge'

Edwards and Mercer (1987) suggest that one of the main purposes of education is to develop a 'common knowledge', a contextual framework for educational activities where the business of 'scaffolding' can take place (p. 161). This is done through joint action and talk, but the nature of that intercourse, though examined by them in educational terms, is not described in terms of emotions. Throughout our research, teachers illustrated their practice in terms of activities and ethos characterized by a variety of feelings. They also described the emotional connections between them and pupil as important in developing common knowledge. Edwards and Mercer's description of 'cognitive socialisation' may be a major function of education but it is affected by the emotional relationships as well.

Theresa's style of teaching includes the generation of excitement and interest, and she uses atmosphere and personal reflection to create this situation. Theresa shows, at the same time, how an emotional connection underpins the child's relationship to his or her work. Her class topic on the Tudors involved looking at plants brought from South America to England by the explorers, constructing Tudor gardens, learning Tudor dances from an outside expert and looking closely at portraits. The work on portraits was used to show how the pictures could be 'read':

> Lucas has put something in his portrait that tells us a great deal about Queen Elizabeth I. He has put in a half sun and some rays coming out of it . . . 'So, if you're finishing your portrait today, how about something in the background to actually show something of the life of this queen or the life of these times, because that background is as equally important as the portrait?'

> *She emphasizes her descriptions of the children's work by slowing her pace and pausing on the 'I love' and the adjectives.*

> I think the portraits are working out splendidly. I think they look marvellous. They look really, really lovely. I love Phil's sorrowful queen, the very pale green face, the arsenic face, and she's looking so sorrowful. I love that contrast between that sorrowful queen and Erica's very, very powerful, buoyant queen up here.

By this time Philip was smiling a little and trying not to look too pleased – he was slightly embarrassed. She then uses the affective power of a poetic style to confirm the importance of what the children are doing and so affecting their involvement.

What does contrast mean? . . . Well done, yes, I love the contrast between this sorrowful queen and this very powerful, very fit healthy queen, and this queen that Phil's done. A queen who is obviously very near to the end of her life, and has kind of caved in, and you wonder if she has caved in under the pressure of all the things she has had to do to keep this country going. All the wars that she has had to fight to keep this country going, all the pressures she has to put up with because she is a woman on the throne, and all these men plotting to take power. It's quite interesting what you can see in these pictures.

All these teachers have provided examples of how they work affectively to be more effective in the learning situation. They generate relationships that feature excitement, interest, enthusiasm, inquiry, excitement, discovery, risk taking and fun. They would agree that learning theories have to be contextualized in a 'cultural forum' where the affective plays a major part (Bruner 1972). The cognitive 'scaffolding' is held together with emotional bonds.

CONCLUSION

The technical-rationalist, market-orientated reforms of the late 1980s and early 1990s regard the teacher as technician and the child as student, as Wendy observes with some vehemence:

I feel the National Curriculum is a completely reductionist approach to education, because it is only subject based. I feel it's a gut reaction on the part of the government to a situation which wasn't honest or right. You're never going to have an ideal situation, but rather than looking at child development and looking at what education should be doing from that point of view, all they do is have a reactive response to what's going on. So they scream to the right, having been for some years on the left. Another few years and they'll be swinging the other way. But no one seems to really look at what child development is, and relate that to education – I mean the inner and the outer world of the child.

The emotions have little place here – indeed they are to be discouraged. Our teachers, however, regarded themselves as professionals and the child as person. Furthermore, they saw themselves as being concerned with the development of the whole person, in contrast to the compartmentalization of knowledge and of child in the National Curriculum. For them, teaching is a moral business first and foremost, in the way Noddings, Tom, Elbaz and others describe. Quite apart from that, however, the child as a student is seen as being dependent on the child as a person in the same way as, for some, the teacher as a teacher is dependent on the teacher's self (Nias 1989). Teaching is a matter of communicating and connecting – through the emotions, through care, trust, respect, rapport. It features a great deal of fun, excitement and enthusiasm. Esteem is important – for self and for others. So is confidence and the removal of fear. Teachers have to unblock children's barriers against the unknowns of secondary socialization before they can proceed, deploying a delicate art in constructing or identifying 'teachable moments'. As with Acker's (1995: 33) teachers, therefore, these teachers are not to be seen as 'unthinking conduits of child-centred ideology or the requirements of the modern state, or as "caring too much"'. They 'made judgements based on experience and according to what worked' (p. 33). This is not a 'Mumsy discourse', but positive pedagogy. They are 'channelling into learning' and servicing 'going with the flow' in a moral enterprise that has a clear vision of the kind of society into which they would wish their pupils to progress.

5

CREATING ATMOSPHERE AND TONE

INTRODUCTION

School ethos has for long been recognized as a highly significant factor in pupil achievement, both in secondary (Rutter *et al.* 1979) and in primary schools (Mortimore *et al.* 1988). The same is true of 'classroom climate', which bred a whole research industry in America following the pioneering work of Lewin, Lippitt and White (1939). Much of this work has been guided by quantitative or experimental research methods, which can establish the framework of significance and its generality without, however, getting to the heart of what school ethos or classroom climate constitutes. For this, we need qualitative methods. In a previous attempt to characterize a particular secondary school ethos through such methods, Woods (1990: 77) conceived of ethos as 'a moving set of relationships within which different groups and individuals are constantly in negotiation. It is expressed largely in symbolic form, notably in language, appearance and behaviour.' In this chapter we seek further characterization of the quality of ethos or climate in relation to primary classrooms.

None of the earlier focus on creative teaching (Woods 1990, 1993, 1995) was on climate. We gradually became aware, however, in this phase of the research, that climate was one of the most prominent features of creative teachers' work. The exceptional events (described in Woods 1993) certainly generated exceptional climates. But there was also a feeling of exceptionality about these teachers' classrooms from day to day outside these events. Much of this was to do with how they created 'atmosphere', and their use of 'tones' in interaction with children to achieve different effects. We came to see atmosphere and tone as important constituents of classroom climate, particularly in the way in which they generated feelings, amongst pupils and teachers alike, conducive to learning. In their effective construction lies the key to what Wendy, earlier (p. 60) called the 'subtle art of teaching'. Theresa comments on how essential she feels this area is, and how underplayed it is in the National Curriculum:

Basically, this is my big bone of contention with the National Curriculum. If you're working in industry you can work by assessing measurable quantities and qualities. We work in a business which is about producing people who can cope, and it's all about immeasurable quantities, immeasurable qualities. You can't overlay your plastic transparency of the National Curriculum, tick it all off and say 'there you are, 16, made a little person there, well done'. You can't do that. We work in a totally subjective atmosphere with subjective qualities and quantities every day. You can't suddenly put objective measurements on top. Yes, you can on very, very simple things, like can this child count up to ten, can this child count to 20. In many ways I've found it quite offensive to the art of actually teaching because it gives it a simplistic quality that it doesn't have.

In this chapter, we try to reconstruct some of the prominent features of the atmosphere of these teachers' classrooms.

CLASSROOM ATMOSPHERE

We have noted the following characteristics: anticipation and expectation, relevance, achievement and success, and satisfaction.

Anticipation and expectation

These teachers are skilled in the construction of situations and their sense of timing:

There's a wooden frame on the carpet with two end supports, a bar across the top with some pulleys hanging from it. The children sit in a circle around it as they arrive and whilst some curious children examine it, most await Grace's introduction and take part in the early morning routines. She doesn't mention it while she deals with the morning jobs and pleasantries.

(Field note)

Visual aids were a common stimulus, as when Laura showed her children some cooking utensils one morning, Eddie showed some materials to make ancient clocks, and Winsome began one morning with a tank full of water by her side. These activities often had a hands-on quality to them, but above all, they heralded 'something new', which was a constant feature. Ira (Year 5), one of Theresa's pupils, commented: 'She likes doing stuff to do with machines, maps and Tudor gardens. She does a lot of imaginative work, a lot of finding out about different times and a lot of experimenting like science and she tries out new stuff from books.'

Exciting out-of-school events, such as trips to museums, art galleries, sporting venues, ancient sites and community projects like film units and arts centres, were eagerly anticipated. New people were often in evidence as teachers used volunteers and invited specialists to assist in particular projects, for example Tudor dance instructors, puppeteers, sports specialists, sculptors. These brought a charismatic quality to the projects in which they took part, as discussed in Woods (1995).

Pupils are often very aware of the extra effort made by teachers to ensure an atmosphere of interest is created. Carla and Sam, Year 5 pupils, describe their perceptions of Wendy's input:

Carla: She can do serious projects which are part of the National Curriculum, but she likes to set up her things which she'd do at the weekend which we were grateful for and you have a laugh with it – like doing little paintings or little origami lessons or something like that which is really good, which she's not really supposed to do. It's not something she's not meant to be doing but it's er hm, she's got her own side. If you went to one classroom they'd have one point of view about what they're doing and she doesn't follow on like a dog on a lead.

Sam: She's not forced to do anything. She's not forced to get special lessons from outside the school.

Carla: She puts herself out for us.

There was also a theatrical quality about the way in which these teachers acted, as noted by Helen, a support teacher, of Grace: 'It's a talent, I suppose, it's a kind of suspense she creates, not all the time, but the children are aware of her at all times in the class . . . It's a lively kind of theatre in a way.'

Relevance

We were able to expand on the importance of relevance, as discussed in an earlier work (Woods 1990). A key aspect of classrooms in the present study was that all identified with and experienced the atmosphere. Pupils felt it, and were moved by it. They felt their experiences were valued, and that they were able to contribute to the world of knowledge being created and explored. Teachers made sure, therefore, that pupils felt a strong sense of involvement. They did this in various ways. Firstly, they used children's personal experiences and interests as part of the curriculum. For example, Wendy encouraged them to draw on family histories to construct evacuation stories, and Thea helped them establish connections with children from a school in Wales:

A suggestion was made to me to look at another locality within the United Kingdom that is different from your own, and it is also a part of the National Curriculum. So we are in the process of doing that. We've written back our second letters and I've taken some photographs. It's a place called Bryncrug, near Tywyn, which is north of Aberystwyth. The children are really keen to carry on next year, so I will ask William [their next teacher] if he will do that.

Nicola found a way to enthuse a child, apparently by accident:

I think, it [chance] probably plays quite a big part in it . . . I didn't know until this child actually started sewing that it was something that he was going to be really good at, and I happened to be walking past him while he was sewing, and I said 'Wow, look at that, isn't that wonderful?' And that's all chance, and then we got talking about it, and I said 'Have you seen my sewing? Because I carry it around with me every day', and he said, 'Oh yeah, this is great and this colour's lovely and that's nice and how did you do that stitch?', and I said 'I'll show you'. It went on from there. That's chance isn't it? I wouldn't have walked into a class and said, 'Hey, have you seen my bit of sewing?' It wouldn't have been a planned thing. I was going to do pattern work with them but in no way was it to do with sewing . . . The sewing was part of the wide range of experiences [and was planned], but it was chance that I went past and made a big deal of it. If I hadn't walked past and done something about it, it might have got left. If I hadn't been interested myself and happened to know a lot about Kaffe Fassett going into prison and getting all the men sewing and the sailors sewing and all that sort of stuff.

Nicola not only shows here how important relevance is to engaging children, she also indicates how her various interests and enthusiasms are relevant to her involvement in her job.

The influence of their teacher in establishing personal relevance is well illustrated by a Year 6 group choreographing part of their musical on their own:

She [Marilyn] talks to the whole group together and then we just tell her our ideas, and other people comment on them and suggest this and that and then we put it all together. She lets us talk about it more than other teachers. She lets us have our own conversations and arguments and then gets us back to the point. She lets us speak, she lets us vote although we're not 18 . . . She lets us breathe more. Most of all she listens, unlike other teachers who jump to conclusions.

Secondly, in relating the curriculum to the pupil, teachers took account of cultural, race, gender and social class distinctions, aiming for a harmonious ethos that is fair to all pupils. As Burwood (1992: 320) argues with respect to improving working-class children's achievement, teachers constantly sought to 'reduce the gap between everyday experience and classroom experience'. Thus, Grace chose to focus her geography topic on a West Indian island because many of her children had West Indian connections and one of her children visited there regularly. Theresa generated discussion on women in public life and emphasized the role Queen Elizabeth I played in supporting women writers. Nathan's Year 2 class focused on similarities and differences between Bangladeshi and English family life in his school, which had a large Bengali population.

A third aspect of relevance is the way learning is related to children's feelings. As Drummond (1991) notes, learning is an emotional enterprise and not solely a cognitive one. Thus, Junior in Laura's class (Year 2), whilst looking at some photographs of his performance in a dance drama, which was the culmination of a term's project on 'worlds', told us that 'I thought I was a fish, swimming like a fish. I thought I was water . . . It was like I was in a picture.' Asked what he enjoyed about doing the dance, he said, 'I like stretching, closing, twisting and skipping and running . . . I liked following the music like I was in the mood.' Junior's use of technical dance language is illustrative of how many of the children in this project picked up the language and used it to help articulate their actions.

Sherene in Grace's class (Year 2) talked about her science book and described clearly how the absence of air causes a flame to go out. When asked what she thought about doing the science she replied, 'fantastic'. She then went on to describe another experiment about sound and the length of tubes – they had made pan pipes. She was then asked again about her feelings towards her book:

> The thing I like about doing this book is that it's all about science and it's really good and you have to do it in your best copy. First you have to do it in your rough copy and then do it in your nice copy like I've just showed you, and when you have done all that you just shade it all in nicer. If I showed this to other teachers they would say it was fantastic and excellent because there is a lot of nice writing and neat drawings. I think this book will be put into achievement assembly because I have put a lot of effort into it.

Sherene and many of her classmates were very enthusiastic about their science activities and proud of their achievements; this definitely appeared to influence their feelings towards science. It would appear to reflect a general improvement in the teaching of science. An inspectorial report on science and mathematics in secondary and primary schools science at the time of the research (OFSTED 1994) concluded that, with the exception of areas such as curricular planning (fitting science into general topics) and the need to improve the science knowledge of teachers (at Years 5 and 6), 'primary science can be counted as a success' (p. 18). Whilst the report refers to the use of 'hands on experiences' being a significant factor, they note that primary science goes beyond this to develop an understanding of important scientific concepts. It also notes that 'Pupils enjoy their science and their motivation can be judged from their sustained interest and concentration' (p. 17).

A fourth feature of relevance is a constant sense of purpose. Theresa explains one way in which this works:

> I want them perhaps to do something with imagination during the day, that's quite important, but most of all, the overriding factor is, sometime during the day you want them to have an end product in their head. One finished thing. If I've got a target, it's that during the day one thing needs to be finished and in their heads. So they go home and someone says 'Right, what did you do today?' as they inevitably do, and they can say I did so and so, I did that today.

Many activities have an end in view that the children recognize. In Theresa's class, the children were asked to construct a vehicle that can roll, design the best leaflet to go home to parents informing them of an outing, write a newspaper report for parents of their sports day, construct flower designs for the harvest festival, simulate the experiences of explorers who first recorded particular flowers discovered in South America by drawing some of them meticulously, and construct a chess board for classroom free time. Wendy's class constructed 'proper' books in which to put their evacuation stories, made puppets for a live performance of a play with a proper theatre, and built sculptures to enhance the school exterior. Thus clear purposes cemented the sense of relevance.

Achievement and success

A feeling of achievement and success is a distinctive feature of the classroom atmosphere. There is a sense of high teacher expectations, and confidence in children's abilities to meet them. Thus, constant encouragement by publicly praising pieces of work is done with the whole class two or three times a day. More informally, the teachers punctuate the various activities by stopping the class to comment on an individual's or a group's work. These public expressions of achievement were often developed by the teacher into a supportive dialogue between members of the class as to the possibility of further enhancing the quality and rigour of the work. Thus, Grace expected her group of children to report back on their science investigation into the use of pulleys to overcome friction, the other children were invited to ask questions and the answers were discussed and evaluated. This approach is related not just to the content of an activity but to developing dialogue as a part of the atmosphere of the classroom. In these interactions the teachers sustained a sense of need for quality. Thus, when one of Eddie's groups had not made much effort to organize a presentation of their clock constructions, they were sent away and given five minutes to re-present their activity. They did so and Eddie described it as a more polished and organized presentation.

This pupil engagement can lead to a collaborative atmosphere of positive encouragement and critique, a kind of 'empathetic challenging' (Bonnett 1991). Marilyn's class at work on book reviews provides an example. After listening to some of the reviews and teacher comments on them in terms of content and depth, the children were then put into groups to listen to each other's reviews and assist in developing them. Here, Lee and Ian comment on Jamie's review which he had just read to them:

Lee: It's like a story isn't it?
Ian: You're telling a story aren't you? At the end you've got 'I like the story, it was interesting.'
Jamie: That's part of the review.
Ian: Yes, but you can't write a story. You've got to think about 'I like the book because [certain] parts happened in it.'
Lee: Yes, you can't write 'I like this book because *all* this is happening.'
Ian: You've got to explain at the beginning what the book is all about. You can't just start with a part of it.
Lee: Yes, and you've got to write down the different characters.

Another of Marilyn's children, Andrew, described how he worked in collaboration with his friend: 'I was with Simon, earlier on over there, we were like a team, weren't we Simon? We were writing, helping each other out by giving each other the answer, by saying "no, that one is two twos equals four, add one is five".' Marilyn, commented:

They're taking a role in teaching themselves. They've learnt something and they can pass it on. There's a huge value for them to know that they have that skill . . . I think it's motivating, it does motivate them because they will look at that [other perspectives and skills] and they will go away and try that or they will try another angle.

She was aware of the risks in this. Children can be 'insensitive', and can 'slip out of [the mutually supportive framework] very easily'. But she based her approach on the conviction that 'deep down there is a caring attitude towards each other and that they have an understanding of learning difficulties and support each other through them'. Her role was important in 'pushing the positive'. In this technique, teachers make a distinction between praise and encouragement. The former may be beneficial in terms of self-esteem but the latter is more directed towards development. Madeline (Year 5) exemplifies this difference in describing her relationship with Theresa:

She really expects us to use our brains, for instance when we did the treasure map with the instructions she said, 'I really want you to think about this, really try and really get somebody else's brain working.' And so she expects us to really put a lot of thought into a piece of work. And I think that if you do something wrong she never really lies. Some teachers lie. If they don't think it's very nice they say, 'Oh that's brilliant'. And they just say that will have to do, but Theresa, if you do something wrong just says, 'OK, that's not very good, go and do it again.' She doesn't say it horribly, 'Oh that's really stupid, go and do it again' . . . When I finish a piece of work you feel like you've achieved something. You know that you've done it and won't have to do it again. If you didn't like it you know that you're finished and you just feel good about it.

All the schools we visited extended classroom achievement to a school level by having weekly achievement assemblies. They would, however, come under the heading of praise rather than encouragement for it was mainly a 'showing' form of assembly with little interaction. Achievement, as Madeline implies, is closely linked to satisfaction.

Satisfaction

Achievement leads to feelings of satisfaction and the sense of 'a job well done', as when Madeline finished her map: 'I felt like it's a whole block of work and . . . I just thought "wow, that's really good" and I did feel quite good about it.' Similarly a great deal of satisfaction is derived from the public display of children's work. Madeline (Year 5) identified what it meant to her:

Well I think, if you look at it up on the wall you say 'that's mine' and 'that's somebody else's' and then you compare them and I think it's nice to look at them because you know what you've done. And if you're just finishing something like that, you look at it on the wall and you can compare them to see if you've progressed.

This confirms the well-known effect of the situation – classroom organization, furnishings, props, displays – on how schoolwork is experienced (for example, Delamont 1976; King 1978). Displays in these classrooms were a prominent component of their atmosphere.

Laura suggests that this sense of satisfaction can be seen on children's faces as a result of being stretched and working hard. Here she refers to a group with whom she is keen to develop their factual and descriptive writing:

We have got quite a good tuition group and they're really being quizzed with their work, about how they're complicating their stories, what sort of resolution they're working towards and where they're going with their work. They're having to work out what their intentions are, and how they can bring all their diverse ideas into it and how they are weaving them all together, and they really are beginning to structure their thinking about it. I'm really pleased. They are complaining a little bit about the amount of work they are having to do, but I actually feel this is a sign of success. There's a sort of self-satisfied thing in there. They say to their mums 'Oh all we ever do is work, work, work, work.' But it's in a rather self-satisfied way. You sort of feel that they are actually quite pleased about it.

THE TONE OF CLASSROOM LIFE

By 'tone' we refer to the sound quality and levels, rhythm, pace and tempo of classroom life. In these respects, an artistic lesson has affinities with a piece of music, with its variations designed for effect, its range of instruments to produce them, and with the teacher as orchestrator and conductor. Different tones produce different moods for different purposes: for example, to generate a particular atmosphere for a story; to construct a state of the emotions, such as seriousness when dealing with an issue of behaviour, or calm or excitement for a particular activity. These tones are often set as soon as the children arrive:

> The children drift in in dribs and drabs in the morning. They get on with reading. Some of them arrived early in order to do this. Theresa greets them with warm humour engaging with each child as they arrive and she teases some of them. She describes them as customers, which amuses them, though they only smile quietly, no one goes over the top or abuses the atmosphere. She describes a music activity and how one of the parents, who is an artist, is coming in to talk to them about their visit to the National Gallery. She jokes about one child's outing money having ruined her washing machine because she left it in her jeans.

Common resources used by teachers are humour and metaphor. There is much warmth conveyed in smiles and twinkles of the eye. Even admonishments are done in this manner. Hera, a fifth-year girl gives an example involving Theresa: 'I did a piece of writing and in the middle I stopped and I found out I'd skipped a line. She kind of put her hand on her hips and kind of pretends to be a bit angry, but really she's just joking while she does make us do it again but, like, she's not furious.'

Metaphors are used constantly, differing ways of describing activities are created, puns are enjoyed, as in this field note: 'Theresa is looking for instructions for a treasure map that are real teasers, "tricky dicky" clues. Clues that need brain power, not hand power. She asks them to create a "state secret".'

Here, we use our own metaphor in trying to convey the main moods identified, likening the lesson to a piece of music. We hope, as Richardson (1994: 519) metaphorically describes metaphor, that 'like the spine' our metaphor 'bears weight, permits movement, is buried beneath the surface, and links parts together into a functional, coherent whole'. It is a 'method of knowing' (p. 520). There are many kinds of moods in creative classrooms. Three prominent ones are those produced by 'andante', 'legato', and 'spiritoso' styles (or tones) of teaching. These differ in both physical and subjective space. In andante style, the teachers usually have the children close to them. In legato, the children spread out into the corridors and use the floors and carpets. In spiritoso, the whole group may be seen at times trailing through the school on an adventure. Even more importantly, perhaps, the varying of the mood is also another way of varying the psychological space. As Harvey (1989: 202) notes, space

> has direction, area, shape, pattern and volume as key attributes as well as distance. We typically treat it as an objective attribute of things which can be measured and thus pinned down. We do recognise of course that our subjective experience can take us into realms of perception, imagination, fiction, and fantasy, which produce mental spaces and maps as so many mirages of the supposedly 'real' thing.

In this way, changes in mood add breadth to a daily learning experience that is generally confined to the more limited space defined by the four walls of a classroom.

Andante *(to be performed in moderately slow time)*

The teacher's aim here is to establish seriousness and to create tension. Rather similar to the 'ripple effect' (Kounin 1970), where humour spreads through a group, so quietness creeps over a group, where a teacher is trying to bring a class to order. Members of the group sensitive to the 'creeping quietness' encourage others to conform; the varied use of stares and mock gestures of disapproval tinged with occasional humour establishes a settled mood among the class. Admonishments to individuals are delivered in quiet whispers so as generally not to embarrass or create martyrs. This does not mean that a soft approach is being used, for whispered, quiet admonishments can be delivered with some considerable conviction and intensity. Individuals are brought into the teacher's 'space'. It rather ensures that a quieter level of interchange is the norm and louder utterances are saved for times of enthusiasm, affirmation and congratulation. Teachers did not keep themselves apart, creating a division between teacher and pupils. They addressed individuals at similar height levels on a one-to-one basis, often with a warm touch of the hand on the arm or shoulder.

Theresa's children often seemed spellbound. She emphasized particular vocabulary, used a slower manner of speaking and deliberate pauses to generate an atmosphere of intensity, excitement, and importance. Her description of Elizabethan times had all the ingredients of mood built up by an andante presentation. Her Year 5 class were due to visit the National Portrait Gallery one afternoon to look at pictures. In the meantime they had been preparing their own portraits of Queen Elizabeth I and making their own scrolls. In this extract, Theresa describes the modern speedy process of making a book, and then goes on to tell the children about printing in Elizabethan times. The children's general hum gradually died down as Theresa leant forward to tell her tale:

She begins in a factual tone emphasizing the 'five years' but it has a 'once upon a time' mood to it.

In Elizabethan days if you wanted a book it had to be copied out by hand and it might take as long as five years to publish it. A man very early on before Elizabethan times had discovered how to print books, William Caxton, but even so, to buy a William Caxton book was extremely expensive and even when it was printed on his machine it took nearly a year to make.

She adds some humour by referring to the shop next to the school.

So you can see you didn't just nip out to Cottingly's Art Shop and buy a paperback for £1.99, you couldn't do that.

Her voice lowers slightly and she slows her delivery, emphasizing 'very, very' and 'fabulously wealthy'.

It is only very, very recently that ordinary people like you and me could go out and say we want a book. Books used to be for the very, very rich.

They were a sign that you were fabulously wealthy and when you look at the portraits this afternoon, you look for what you see behind those portraits, because what you see behind those faces of the people in the pictures, those are the stories that tell you about the people in those pictures.

The story takes on a poetic style in the way she uses consecutive negatives.

Not the false faces that the artist has given them, not the flattery that the artist has been paid to do, but you look behind those pictures and you see the real Elizabethan life. You will see the books which say 'I am filthy rich. I can afford books.'

Here she uses the word 'look' three times. Her voice quickens as she emphasizes the 'born, live and die'. And then she pauses before continuing.

Look at the land. That tells you that these people ruled the land. Look at the clothes. Look at the maps and it tells you that these people travelled. Until very recently, the last 150 years, people expected to be born, live and die in one place and if these people were travelling it was because they were fabulously wealthy and powerful. You look at what's behind those pictures, behind those people and behind those very, very serene faces, a lot of which have got nothing to do with the real people behind them.

'Real' is the next word to be emphasized and she brings the metaphor of the detective to help put the children in control of the afternoon activity. There is a long pause after 'lies' and nobody interrupts. She uses the lists to help create the mood.

Look for the clues this afternoon. Be the detective when you look at those pictures, because that's where real Elizabethan England lies. Look behind those pictures and you'll see dogs, animals, horses, not mongrel dogs, but pedigree hunting dogs, fabulous Arabian horses, because behind those people are their very precious possessions. You know that in ancient Egypt the pharoahs were buried with their precious possessions, yeah!

She brings in the Egyptians to prove her point, knowing that the children know about them.

In Elizabethan England, in portrait painting, possessions were put behind people to show, just like the Egyptians, how powerful they were. Egyptians took their belongings to their grave. People from the Elizabethan age, the Victorians, the Stuarts, took their possessions to the grave with them, in the pictures they left.

She finishes by including the pupils in the repetitive 'we know'.

We know exactly who they were, we know exactly where they stood, we know exactly what power they had, because it's there in the pictures, yeah.

Both researcher and children were entranced by the richness of the language, the poetic construction and the clear images. Theresa is sure that the creation of mood is an important part of her craft:

Capturing the audience is a difficult thing in teaching, isn't it? It's this elusive thing students call discipline . . . it's the captivation, it's creating a pause, and then bang in on the pause. It's the pause where J.P.R. Williams would have nipped in, picked up the ball and been off, it's that sort of change of direction, skidding off one surface and on to another. It's that which you're creating, it's capturing the audience . . . in the palm of your hand. You're doing basically what an entertainer or performer does. If you actually analyse what a stand-up comic does, it's very akin to what a teacher does.

Here, Theresa refers to the art of 'timing', such an important ingredient of the comedian's skill, which Eisner (1979) feels is intrinsic to the artistic teacher's role. There is also a sense of emotional as well as cognitive engagement of the audience, so that all are captured in a spirit of *communitas* (Woods 1993). Theresa finally comments on her role as facilitator, building on children's own experiences in giving them an emotional charge towards new knowledge:

> It's the same with the Tudors and Stuarts when you talked of me creating excitement. It's about me creating this all-powerful, almost fable queen, like fable King Alfred, mystical things that children read in books. It's them latching on to it, it's not really the excitement I've given them. It's the vocabulary that I've given them that gets them to home in on what they've found exciting somewhere else.

Legato (smoothly and connectedly, no gaps or breaks)

This tone was adopted as the general working atmosphere of the classroom. It had a steady rhythm which the teacher occasionally slowed down to emphasize something of importance. Pupils had more personal space and time than in andante, being given more control of their activities, and working in small groups or as individuals, rather than as the whole class under the teacher's direction. Thus, when Theresa's children were creating their portraits of Queen Elizabeth I, there was a quiet buzz as they went about their work, some on their own, some together. They showed initiative in finding tools, space on corridor floors and in the classroom, and in starting work. As the activity progressed, there was a steady movement as pupils stepped over each other to borrow items, but mostly they stayed in their selected space purposefully engaged in the detail of their own activity. Sometimes they sought help from or assisted each other. One child, usually chatty, whistled quietly to herself as she did some extended detailed work. A group of six talked quietly, mostly in relation to task. This all contributed to the sense of a 'working noise' (Woods 1983: 136). The teacher was constantly on the move, orchestrating from within the class, moving from site to site, keeping the rhythm and smooth pace going. She constructed a sentence with Philip, advised a group on a colour, knelt down to assist Tom, validated another child's writing as 'authentic Elizabethan', now engaging with a group at desk level, now sitting in a spare chair talking to an individual about their work, anxieties, or behaviour, and now bringing the class closer, metaphorically speaking, by commending somebody's efforts out loud.

It is in this legato mode that the tone is set for inquiry and dialogue. Wendy, in describing the construction of a script for a puppet show the children were producing, noted that where they had to work as a group, 'they enjoyed building up their dialogue with each other, and came out with some really good, interesting, funny dialogue, and learnt it all.' In another example, Theresa established a legato tone in which a constant dialogue was heard emanating from all the groups, as her class of 7-year-olds constructed their publicity about a trip to Brighton. She suggested that they took on the role of travel agents. They had to decide, in groups, how much money to take with them. Then they planned a letter to their parents about the outing. Some wrote the letter, others suggested what they should take with them and others designed the front cover. The groups tackled the task in their own way. Theresa brought some examples to the attention of the whole class and new ideas or methods were generated amongst the whole class. This is typical of legato mood, in the profusion of ideas, involving children in some practical or investigative activity, with close attention to language and vocabulary.

Spiritoso (with spirit)

A spiritoso tone, involving animation, vigour and liveliness, generates a mood of excitement, joy, interest and enthusiasm. There is much humour and many smiling faces. This tone is commonly used to 'arouse appetite' (Hargreaves 1983), for example stimulating the whole class in a unifying venture such as an assembly, or in preparation for activities, or for effect in telling stories. There is often a quicker pace, more noise, and more variation in pitch than in other styles.

The celebration phase of critical events (Woods 1993) is often characterized by such a mood. Such was the case here with the preparation by some sixth-year children of a musical based on a story of Henry VIII and his six wives as the culmination of a term's topic on the Tudors. The pupils decided who was to play each part, and contributed some choreography and musical compositions. They were excited at the thought of performing, even more so because they were all dressed in very elaborate Elizabethan costumes. The classroom was a hive of activity as last-minute amendments were made to the costumes by the teacher, Marilyn, and a parent governor. There was lots of calling out 'Look at me!' and other humorous comments, accompanied by much giggling. As they were on their way to perform it to their parents they were asked about their feelings. They all seemed to have a high charge of adrenalin. Michael was 'looking forward to the cheering and the laughter and my mates trying their very hardest and their very best'. Nicola was excited and said she felt 'good, lovely' and laughed loudly. She was 'looking forward to getting the whole play right and nothing wrong'. She was 'nervous . . . But after I've done it, I'll probably want to do it again.' Georgina spoke with a large grin over her face. She felt she was 'looking forward to doing it, I don't know why, but I am, although I don't want to do it. I'm frightened of getting one bit wrong, but I still want to do it.' Wayne said he would overcome his nervousness by 'just carrying on and not thinking about it'. He became so overcome with emotion during his solo – he told us so later – that he began to cry. However, he did carry on, with everyone in the hall willing him to finish his song. As they lined up to go in, some called out excited comments about other characters' costumes and roles. Gradually, Marilyn lowered her voice and paused more often, using a more andante tone. Eventually, the children came to order and gracefully descended the stairs holding hands in Tudor style to begin their performance. They were quiet and, as exemplified in their comments, full of contrasting emotions of nervousness and excitement.

The teacher also becomes carried along with the excitement her planned activities generate. Thea reported how she had been reading about 'Til Owlyglass' who 'gets up to all sorts of mischief and the children adore it'. She had told them, 'I can't wait to read this to you. I took it home at the weekend and I read it and couldn't put it down.' Thea's enthusiasm was taken up by the children and the story became valued because of the feelings of excitement their teacher generated in the children for her story. The content and presentation of the story was not the only stimulus to interest.

CONCLUSION

Teachers' and pupils' emotional involvement in teaching and learning, has not figured prominently in government educational policy of late. Rather, during the 1980s and 1990s, it has been marked by an increasing emphasis upon rationality in teaching, the close delineation of ends to be achieved, summative assessment with which to measure success, and bureaucratic structures and processes with which to monitor the system. Teaching is in danger of losing its emotional heart, even more so since, in the preoccupation with cognition, it has never been properly identified. The same might be said for learning. However, some teachers, at least, are still managing to cultivate what they consider to be the 'subtle art of teaching'. Through the artful construction of atmosphere, teachers imbue pupils with the desire to learn, with the feeling of deep personal involvement and purpose, and with a sense of strong intrinsic rewards. They create and sustain moods appropriate to the task in hand through the skilful deployment of a variety of tones, which make subtle use of time and space. Jackson (1992: 90) argues that we must look at the minutiae of school life through an interpretative frame, cultivating a 'heightened sensitivity to the nuances of schooling'. Atmosphere, tone, mood are hardly minutiae, but they do contain some significant nuances. It is in this area that teachers give an 'aesthetic form to their existence through their own productive work' (Foucault 1979). We have tried to indicate the potential fruitfulness of this area, and of the qualitative approach to its study, in seeking to understand some of the more intangible, but highly significant, constituents of the art of teaching.

6

STIMULATING THE IMAGINATION THROUGH STORY

The genuine storyteller must feel the urgency to divulge what it
means to live in an age when many lies pass for truth in the mass
media and the public realm. The storyteller must contrast the
social reality with a symbolic narrative that exposes contradictions.
From this contrast, the storyteller gives birth to light and sheds
light on the different ways in which children can become their own
storytellers.

(Zipes 1995: 14)

Encouraging children to think for themselves, to see from the point of view
of others, to be productive in ideas, to feel and to empathize with others
– in short, to be imaginative – was high on our teachers' agenda. Maxine
Greene (quoted in Egan and Nadaner 1988) considers the imagination
an 'instrument of liberation'. Without it, we get 'intellectual paralysis'.
This is exactly what the National Curriculum achieved in the early stages.
There was no room for imagination. Creativity was not required (Elliott
1991). Egan (1992) argues that imagination should be pervasive throughout education. He conceives of it, not as a particular part of the mind, but
rather as a 'particular kind of flexibility, energy and vividness that comes
from the ability to think of the possible and not just the actual, and which
can imbue all mental functions . . . It makes all mental life more meaningful; it makes life more abundant' (p. 65). Education certainly involves some
accumulation of knowledge and skills, but education can be much more
than this. Imagination enables critical evaluation of the knowledge, to see
beyond and around it, appropriation of it to one's self, transcendence
of the conventional. Imagination stimulates the meanings the learner is

continually having to ascribe to what has to be learned. 'The more flexibly we can think of things as possibly being, so the richer, and the more unusual and effective can be the meanings we compose' (p. 51). Creative teachers might be expected to produce creative learners. Our teachers certainly had this aim in view, as is evident from previous chapters.

THE IMPORTANCE OF NARRATIVE

Howe and Johnson (1992) highlight the importance of narrative and story to children's lives and to their learning processes. They show that there are many types of narrative such as argument, account, story, legend and biography, and that they differ in terms of form, length, source and content. Howe and Johnson (1992) argue that stories and storytellers are everywhere, 'at the breakfast table, on the bus or train, in the playground and workplace, in the pub, at the party, over tea, before bedtime and just as potently in our dreams' (p. 3). Stories help form a bridge between home and school, for 'Home is a place where stories are told. This is a fundamental definition of home which is not in the dictionaries. A family lives by its stories. Without them it is without past and without future, without imagination, without vision, without aspirations' (Wilkinson *et al.*, quoted in Howe and Johnson 1992: 3).

This is why the story helps 'bring home' to the child the content of the curriculum, and establishes 'common knowledge' (Edwards and Mercer 1987). Salmon goes further, suggesting that to live is to be in a narrative:

Each of us lives in a story that is ours alone. It is this story which gives our lives their essential shape, defines their heights, their plateau, their declines, marks out their movements, direction, changes in direction. In living, we tell our own stories. Nor are these stories merely a catalogue of events which occur within our life span. As the authors of our own personal story, it is we who must select from the myriad happenings we witness daily, what belongs to the story and what lies outside. Only we can weave what we select into the narrative, only we ourselves can link what is happening now with what has passed, and what may yet happen in our lives. As authors we have agency.
(Salmon quoted in Howe and Johnson 1992: 4–5)

In consequence, Howe and Johnson argue that 'young people arriving in school already possess a "deep structure" of story – a recognition of it and an ability to use it in many different ways in their learning.' Egan (1992: 64) notes other aspects of its pedagogical value:

The development of the narrative capacities of the mind, of its ready use of metaphor, of its integration of cognitive and affective,

of its sense-making and meaning-making, and of its over-arching imagination, is of educational importance because these capacities are
so central to our general capacity to make meaning out of our own
experience and of the world we find ourselves in.

There are key differences between adults and children in terms of
thought: 'Whereas adults differentiate their thought with specialised
kinds of discourse such as narrative, generalisation, and theory, children
must, for a long time, make narrative do for all' (Moffett 1968, quoted in
Fox 1989: 25).

Thus children when they begin school already know a lot about stories, how they are constructed, what to expect and how to respond. They
know the questions to ask because of their experience of doing it (Howe
and Johnson 1992: 4). Egan (1988) also argues that children already have
some skills and knowledge about narrative and its form when they are at
this stage, and that their imagination is quite sophisticated. For example,
they have a good understanding of the form and content of traditional
stories such as Cinderella and other folk tales. Egan (1988) maintains
that young children's use of narrative is similar to the Homeric tradition
of orally transmitted stories that contain the history and culture of an
epoch. In his analysis of this tradition he describes how the stories of
Homer were able to be passed on due to the rhythmic patterns, not of the
text, but of orality itself. He asserts that the developmental and experiential approach – from the concrete to the abstract, from the unknown to
the known – limits our understanding of children's capabilities because
the approach ignores children's imaginative skills.

Our teachers were observed encouraging and developing a wide variety
of types of storytelling. We shall consider their use of narrative and stories,
and their chief pedagogical means – through encouraging pupils' work
with books and reading, and through talk.

STORIES AND NARRATIVES

From the time that pupils come to school at 5 years old or below, stories
are a major feature. Every morning when pupils in our schools entered
their classroom, new and old stories were unfolded. Teachers told stories,
created stories, imported stories, played a part in a story, and took children in search of stories. The stories involved characters, events, arguments, visions and emotions. Teachers used stories to teach, to respond
to life as a story and to understand the importance of valuing each individual's story. They invited stories from the children during the morning
welcome session, for example, describing a child's religious festival. They
told humorous stories from their own lives concerning their washing
machine or their cat. They used a story about a trip round Sainsbury's as

the basis for a maths lesson. They read numerous stories, discussed the characters, the issues – for example, how some children from an urban school rejected a traveller girl, or the story of how an old man faced death. They introduced a lesson in which the children had to do a mathematical transposition of a figure of a giant and then discuss the character, clothes and environment the children's giant might inhabit. They asked the children to explore their families' history of the war and evacuation or other similar journeys and encouraged them to construct their own imaginative story of the events. They took them on outings and told stories of lost children. Children's reports of their outings were made into books and they were invited to bring into school memorabilia from home and tell stories about them.

Georgina (Year 6) brought in some of her father's boxing medals and a discussion arose concerning the pros and cons of boxing. Ben (Year 2) brought in a violent comic which Laura did not like, and she gently said so. Dean confidently said '*I* do', and its qualities were debated. This involvement of personal narratives with school legitimizes pupil and family knowledge. Further, teachers valued popular culture. For example, in Marilyn's class, children had a special session each week to bring in what reading materials they liked, and a popular 'keep fit' video was experienced as part of a PE programme. As was noted earlier, Theresa took her children to an Arsenal football match, and encouraged the pupils to talk about what they knew about the team and its performance, again legitimating personal and prior knowledge.

Teachers brought in newspaper articles about anti-racism and encouraged their children to recount stories of racism that then become part of the classroom knowledge. They told graphic stories of past heroines, such as Elizabeth I (see Chapter 5), and enthusiastically praised pupils who captured the spirit of a character in their written and artistic work. The occasional classroom conflict, the poor tidying-up session, an unsuccessful completion of a task, a disappointing music lesson become yesterday's stories, to be interpreted and examined, and were not the basis for stereotyping the class or any individual as uncooperative or lazy. This contrasts with other research (Pollard 1985), that shows teachers using a good deal of stereotyping. These teachers were conscious of the limits and dangers of stereotyping (see Chapter 7), and they actively countered any such inclinations.

There are many different kinds of stories – differences in form, length, source, content – and they have many different outcomes. Storytelling ranges from anecdote – the personal story that often illustrates argument – through traditional storytelling, to the stories told in non-fiction books. However, all these types of story have narrative as a common characteristic. Two prominent kinds used by our teachers were personal, and issue-related stories.

Personal narratives

Narratives, particularly oral narratives, play a big part in influencing class-room atmosphere. Teachers appreciate and challenge personal narratives, describe and evaluate narratives relating to new knowledge or classroom activities, and examine narratives relating to social, moral and political issues. Teachers' anecdotes are often family-based. Marilyn, when intro-ducing her discussion on anti-racism, told her sixth-year pupils that her daughter went to the same school as a black teenager allegedly murdered in a racist attack. She also told the children how her son and his black friend both had to endure racist taunts and jibes when they were out together.

> You know my son Matthew, well, he's 16 and his best friend Amin is black, and Amin comes round every morning and they go to school together. They do everything together. They're both very big so they can look after themselves, but do you know what is really, really sad is that there are people who are both black and white who object to the fact that they are friends. They are being taunted by white boys, they've been taunted by black boys because they are one white and one black and they are good friends. The white people have said 'you don't want to be friends with him, he's a . . .', and the black boys have said to Amin 'you don't want to be friends with him'. They have actually had to run sometimes from groups of boys. It worries me terribly. It worries me as a mum. I'm really very, very pleased that they are friends but there is something terrible in this that worries me. It's not our fault that Amin is black and Matthew and him are together. I like Amin, but it's a terrible feeling that I have to come to terms with all the time and I keep thinking about it when they go out somewhere.

Theresa described what Christmas meant to her by telling the chil-dren about her Christmas dinner before asking the children to write about what it meant to them. She also used a personal experience to address a misdemeanour. Some of her Year 5 pupils had dropped out of a French class without having the courtesy to tell the French teacher. As a related narrative to the issue she was addressing with the children – that of per-sonal responsibility – Theresa read out a letter she had written to an ad-viser apologizing profusely for forgetting an appointment. The atmosphere was quite tense as she unravelled her narrative and her feelings of shame in forgetting the appointment. Laura, when discussing the construction of the class's giant and its short leg, told the children that her son had one leg shorter than the other and he 'managed OK'.

Teachers encouraged anecdotes that reinforced the narrative mode. Stephanie (Year 2) came in one morning with a story about her mother having pulled a tooth out. The story was told in graphic detail and other children were asked to recount their experiences.

During this, a classroom assistant – Sylvia – joined in using humour and developed the narrative:

> Can I just tell you a little story about somebody with a tooth that fell out in the playground? His tooth had come out and another boy had got it, and I said, 'Where's your tooth then? Come on, and I'll put it in a tissue for you.' He said 'Oh, he's got it 'cos he's gonna take it round his dad's 'cos they get more money round there' (*laughter*).

Laura argued that in developing the imagination it is possible also to generate critical inquiry and that the latter is essential for science and maths as well as for the more aesthetic curriculum:

> You've obviously got some sort of perimeter because of the sort of classroom situation, but to really truly develop the imagination you've got to let them go where they need to go, where their imagination takes them and you've got to support it and you've got to enhance it and you've got to illuminate it and you've got to tie the ends up for them.

She recounted how she had to explain to her governors how important this was

> It was like I'd dropped a bomb that had gone off in silence when I said that we have to educate their imagination so that they're using their imagination in maths and science, and it wasn't something that you just did in art or just in creative writing. They thought developing the imagination appropriate but that it had nothing to do with science and maths.

The tooth-pulling narrative shows clearly how teachers develop children's imagination and generate critical inquiry. After Sylvia's story, which had in turn been stimulated by some of the children's narratives about getting money for teeth, the children showed how they recognized the narrative form and they joined in the story by exaggerating their experiences. Jenny developed this, firstly in a humorous manner:

Thomas:	I was in bed last night and my tooth fell out and I got four pounds and a fiver.
Jenny:	Four pounds and a fiver. Here pass the pliers!
Laura:	I'll go and get the pliers.
Jenny:	Here it comes! Get rid of that one and I'll have nine pounds for it.

A number of questions were raised by both the children and the teachers during this discussion, which required some intellectual problem solving.

They compared amounts of money found under their pillows, discussed how it got there, whether the 'tooth fairy' was real, how she would carry her money. The group investigated the hypothesis suggested by one of the children that the teeth that disappear from under the pillow are recycled – this concept was part of the topic they were doing at the time – as new teeth for future babies:

Lee:	Laura, when my teeth came off I was eating an apple and my tooth just came out and I went out to my door, my front door, and tried to throw it up the air. Then I found it again and I put it in my tissue, and I put it in my purse, and then I put my purse back in my pillow and then there was no money in there when I woke up.
Laura:	Why do you think that was?
Lee:	Because they couldn't see it.
Kayleigh:	You have to put it under your pillow and you have to wrap it in sellotape or something and they have to see it.

Logical solutions are being tried out by the children in response to the problems posed in each others' narratives.

Laura:	They have to see it, do they? Right. What about this tooth fairy then, does the tooth fairy have anything to do with it? What do you think, Shareen?
Shareen:	The big money is too big for the fairies' pockets.
Laura:	So if the big money is there it's from your mum is it? Shareen thinks that the tooth fairy has only got little pockets.

Logical answers to the problem of small pockets are offered and then a fantasy answer is suggested.

Shareen:	They can only put 5p in their pockets.
Laura:	Not four pounds and a fiver.
Lola:	They can make it up in fives.
Natalie:	Jenny, they can wrap it up and can make it into a little stone and make it smaller and they can then put it in their little purse.
Jenny:	Then they make it big again.
Leyla:	They can unfold it and then put it under your pillow.
Kayla:	They can't unfold the metal, they can't fold metal money up.
Authony:	Where does all the money come from?

This question gets lost in the general discussion but it shows that the children also pose problems.

Laura:	Well, Ashley, excuse me, can I just mention one thing that I'd like you to think about? Aren't fairies supposed to have something to do with magic?
Children:	Yes.
Laura:	Sorry, Rosa?
Rosa:	They turn the money back into big money.
Kayla:	No, they turn the teeth into money.

Alternative explanations are explored based on knowledge about second teeth.

| Laura: | Ah, now that's an interesting idea. Turn the teeth into money. What do you think about that Ashley? |
| Ashley: | No, I don't think so. My mum told me that they take the teeth away and they give you the money and then when a new baby's born, they come back to your house when it's time for their teeth to come up and they are your teeth that are used. |

Another new narrative is introduced. All of these narratives develop out of the class topic of worlds and the environment.

Laura:	Really, is that what happens to all the old teeth, they all get recycled?
Natalie:	No, they come back to you, they do.
Laura:	How can your baby teeth come back to you?
Natalie:	My mum got her teeth back.
Jenny:	Natalie, Natalie, Natalie, how did your mother get her teeth back?
Natalie:	It's just grown again.
Laura:	Really?

These examples show how the adults, Laura, Jenny and Sylvia accept the mixture of fantasy and reality narrated by the children. It is done in a light-hearted, ironic way, which most of the children recognize because they smile at the adults' comments, and smile when they talk. The children take a creative part in this narrative by raising the stakes with the amount of money put under pillows. Nevertheless the adults are working in the 'zone of proximal development' (Vygotsky 1978) in the way they pose problems for them to address. The children are encouraged not only to narrate their stories but to speculate as to how to solve the practical and theoretical problems of money appearing and being carried and how they know that fairies exist.

Issue-related narrative

Egan (1992) argues that social virtues such as tolerance and justice follow from the development of the imagination. It enables a 'transcendence' of

our 'conventional sense of the "other"' (p. 54), and enables us to put ourselves in the place of others, and thus enhances our understanding in a
'heartfelt' way. Stories are particularly good because 'the story not only
conveys information and describes events and actions, but because it also
engages our emotions' (p. 55). It displays qualities in a way that makes
them part of ourselves.

In this type of discussion, the class is usually together. Either an issue
arises from within the teacher's plans or it arises spontaneously. Most of
the teachers made it their business to tackle both public and private issues.
However, concern for wider issues is also a significant feature of these
teachers' work, and narrative is a predominant method for addressing
them. Thus Theresa wove gender issues into her work on Elizabeth I (see
Chapter 2). Grace ensured that the differences between poor and rich life
were brought out in her topic on St Lucia by referring to photographs,
and treated them as narratives to be interpreted. Laura tackled pollution
by reading a related story about the dying Earth and got the children to
discuss the causes and consequences. She investigated the subject of bul-
lying, which arose spontaneously, encouraging the children to describe
their own experiences. When a child brought in some photographs of
herself and some friends at the London Dungeon – a museum concerned
with torture and executions – Laura firstly discussed with her class what
frightened them. She then went on to talk about truth and fiction using
television programmes as a resource. She had asked them the previous
week to look at the news and after this discussion she went on to talk
about television news of Nelson Mandela being inaugurated as South
Africa's President. On a subsequent occasion, she got her Year 2 children to narrate details of things they had done that they subsequently
felt sorry about.

All of these were done in a narrative form. Laura took up the subject
of smoking with her Year 2 pupils when it occurred in a class session. She
firstly dealt with the facts of the issue by establishing with the children
from their observations what is detrimental about smoking. Then she
brought in personal narratives to enhance the conceptualization of the
smoking process:

> Your lungs can get black. Do you know I actually knew a doctor who
> used to work in a place called Wales. And in Wales they used to have
> lots of coal mines. Do you remember when we talked about that black
> rock that people burn and the men who dig the coal out get lots of
> black dust inside their lungs, and this doctor said that it looks just
> like they've been smoking a lot, with all the dirt that went inside their
> lungs.

She then alighted on a specific child's comment and developed the
issue in relation to their personal experiences and anecdotes:

Natalie: When you smoke it doesn't only make your lungs dirty, it makes the air dirty as well.

Laura: That's right . . . So other people who are in the room, what effect does it have on them?

Personal narratives included some about parents smoking in the bathroom, in the car and close to the children even when they were ill. There was much laughter over Natalie's experience: 'We've got a smoke alarm and my mum set off the fire alarm.' Laura then asked them their opinion about being 'smoked over' and Natalie mixed her opinion with narrative: 'I say "Mum, if I find out you've smoked I'm going to be really angry." She promised that when we got back from holiday she would stop smoking, and when we got back from Lanzarote she did, and now she doesn't smoke any more.'

The session petered out. Laura didn't feel she had to make a moral point about smoking, and she didn't ensure that the group came to a significant conclusion. Neither did she demand scientific explanations or justifications in terms of evidence to substantiate belief. Bonnett (1991) argues that rational-calculative versions of thinking always ask for evidence and argument to determine truth. They develop thinking through a movement away from value and unsupported belief, towards more specific reasoned knowledge: 'The goal of thinking is knowledge and knowledge is defined as belief which is not only true but accurate and based on good reasons' (p. 278). Bonnett argues that this approach leads children to thinking about things, and in turn to things deriving their meaning from the place they are allocated in our system of categories of public knowledge. The function of thinking becomes mastery. His alternative approach, particularly evidenced in primary teaching is 'poetic thinking', where instead of mastering reality, reality is revealed through a direct relationship with things themselves which is receptive to their uniqueness. He suggests that poetic thinking leads to authenticity of thought 'wherein individuals make what they have learnt their own by coming to feel its value in the context of their own real concerns, i.e. concerns for the expression of which they accept personal responsibility' (p. 284).

Laura shows, alongside other teachers in this chapter, how she was concerned to ensure that public knowledge is experienced through personal interests. This was done by prioritizing time for exploration of these various issues through narrative. Narratives from the children were interspersed with Laura's narratives concerning her smoking habits, and connections made with miners' illnesses. Laura's personal views on smoking are probably evident to us, but she did not overtly indicate her view, though her line of questioning might be interpreted as clear evidence. However, the point is that this form of narrative exchange is a regular feature of these classrooms, and the example shows how the children easily respond to that form.

In another example from Marilyn's class, Georgina, a Year 6 pupil, described two stories concerning racism. One involved her mother being harassed when she was trying to vote in an election; the other was about the death of a woman whilst the police were making attempts to deport her. Other stories arising in the same session included one in which a white girl in the class explained how she had to be sent away to her grandmother's because her father feared for her safety after he had intervened to protect an Asian family from a racist assault on the estate where they lived. These stories led to an examination of Nazism during the discussion lasting an hour. As the discussion drew towards the end, Georgina asked Marilyn about an incident in the school where the headteacher had told the school at assembly about a famous sculpture she had seen which was so horrible she had decided not to bring pictures of it into the school. The sculpture was a black figure with goggles on. Marilyn became caught up in the discussion concerning her own subjective reactions (she studied art at college):

Michael: Miss Jones said in assembly she had seen this animal and she said it was so black that she couldn't bring it into school because it might scare everyone.

Marilyn: I don't think she said it quite like that ...

Children (all together):   Yes she did.

Georgina: She said it was so black it reminded her of Stevie Wonder and it was too black she couldn't bring it into school, it might scare everybody.

Marilyn: I've seen that, I've seen what she's talking about actually. That is a very, very interesting point. Have you seen it?

Michael: No.

Marilyn: It's a sculpture but it's just a bust.

Georgina: Miss, why can't she bring it in, then?

Marilyn: It's by a very famous sculptor and it's a black shoulders and head.

Kim: Portrait?

Marilyn: Yes, and it's got these golden goggles and it's a very strong sculpture and I don't, I don't know.

Marilyn talks very slowly at this point picking her words carefully. But John, a white boy, seems to spot her reticence and asks her a direct question.

John: Does it scare you?

Marilyn: Does it scare me?

Michael: No.

Michael tries to guess her response. Marilyn responds cautiously but she takes the discussion seriously and answers honestly.

Marilyn: I found it intimidating actually. It was . . .
Michael: Scary?

This is testing the teacher. The teacher is 'put on the line'.

Marilyn: In a way, yes, it was, sort of. This is a very, very
interesting issue . . . because what you're saying is
challenging my thinking about what I'm seeing. I'm
wondering what I felt about it now and why I felt like it.
I think the way I felt about it was about the eyes. What it
has. . . .
Michael: It's got no eyes.
Marilyn: That's right, it hasn't got eyes. That's what I mean. I
don't like people wearing those sort of sunglasses where
I can't see their eyes when you're talking to them.
Michael: I wear them and everyone looks frightened.

*This is said a little cheekily but Marilyn carries on. By addressing this seriously,
she is maintaining the dialogue and introducing new issues to consider.*

Marilyn: Yes, I don't like it. I don't like not seeing eyes.
Georgina: Why not?
Marilyn: Why not? Because as Shakespeare put it, they are 'the
window to your soul'. If I talk to you, I look into your
eyes.
Michael: You can look into the glasses, then.
Georgina: Yes, but Miss, if it was very, very, very white and it had
golden goggles on it would it scare you?

*Georgina brings the subject back to what she has seen as racism. Marilyn is
nonplussed, and then confirms their role as critical learners.*

Marilyn: A very interesting point, that really is. That is a very,
that's interesting . . . You see this is what you should be
doing. You should be challenging the way people think.
You're challenging the way I think now because I
wonder what I'm seeing when I see that or why I think
that. I've got a picture of it. It's not the actual sculpture.
I'll look for it and try and bring it for you to look at it
and see what it is.
Milton: It won't worry me.
Marilyn: No, no, no, art is very emotive. It makes you feel things,
doesn't it?

*Allowing the initial discussion on racism to go on has uncovered this incident in
the school and also led to art becoming the main topic. This not only shows the
dominance of the narrative form but shows the multiple nature of narratives and
their connections.*

Marilyn indicates her approach to discussions around issues:

I suppose that's all built into this thing of expectation and the structures in the classroom. I have decided to have very flexible boundaries. They now have an expectation that I will try to answer their
questions honestly to the best of my ability, and I'm not afraid to say
to them 'I really don't know, I don't know where to begin with that,
I'll tell you what I think or what I believe', but I don't set myself up
to be an all-knowing sort of person. They do have that expectation
that I will answer them.

Teachers intentionally brought issues into their classrooms. In doing so,
they were ensuring the classroom curriculum remained relevant to their
pupils. These 'circular communication' sessions, whether engaging with a
specific curriculum investigation, or having arisen out of personal experiences, or out of issues, are considered by Coles (1994) to be ones in which
the teacher as an authoritarian gives way to the teacher as a mediator. He
suggests that the teacher role is to be one in which she insists on rigorous
rational procedures and avoids idle conversation. Whilst agreeing with his
general tenet concerning talk, the example above shows how the pupils
themselves can be the ones to insist on rationality, and that conversations
between teachers and pupils can be very productive in classrooms where
teachers believe that the pupils can make significant contributions to the
exploration of the world. The examples may not relate directly to a curriculum plan, but still have a large contribution to make to pupil development. They are natural discourses, and the structures the pupils use to
interpret these issues and experiences are the same structures they need
to explore the cognitive world of the sciences and of the arts. According to Vygotsky (1978), every function of children's cultural development
appears twice; first on a social level, and later at an individual level. All
higher functions originate as actual relations between human individuals.
We turn now to consider the chief means of engaging with stories – through
books and talk.

THE USE OF BOOKS

A significant feature of our teachers' classrooms was the large amount of
time spent on reading. To gain some quantitative idea of this, we mon-
itored the amount of class time spent on four areas: tasks, class sessions,
school assemblies, and reading activities. This was done in three classes
over three consecutive days in each class. The reading category included
being read to by the teacher. On the results of a three-day systematic ob-

servation of these three teachers, two of them, Laura and Marilyn spent around 24 per cent of the classroom time on set reading sessions, and Grace around 11 per cent. All the classrooms we observed had a large range of attractive books prominently displayed and they all had set 'quiet reading' times. On top of this, books played a large part in the daily classroom life. Children brought in their own reading material, books went home regularly, parents were invited to attend discussions on reading, special displays of particular authors were constructed and book reviews played a major part in the daily routine. It was often difficult for the teachers to get the children to put the books down. Even if their reading ability was limited, they often discussed the illustrations. They were encouraged to discuss their interests with the teacher, the class or group, and not only were their interpretations publicly acknowledged, but perspectives, issues and opinions were shared.

Laura describes why she thinks books are important to her Year 2 children, and provides an illustration of enthusiasm from one of those children who often would not put his book down:

> Well, they're little worlds that they can enter. They can sort of travel around in them. They can be part of them. People are part of the stories in different ways. You ask children sometimes, 'Were you in this story? Did you think of yourself as being in this story? If you were in this story were you somebody else or were you being this person?' . . . It's a sort of virtual reality. Maybe we didn't need [modern film and computer] virtual reality, maybe we already had it. They're taking their experiences into the book and interpreting the book according to what they know. So they need to ask questions sometimes because their experience doesn't make sense of what's in the book. Especially when you see children like Anthony, who clearly is not an efficient decoder of word, yet he is now learning to enjoy reading time. His favourite book at the moment is a recipe book. We all like recipe books, don't we? And he loves it.

There were a number of features of working with books that, we would argue, added to the pupils' feelings of control over the curriculum. Firstly, the regular daily handling of books enabled children to feel some control over school knowledge. They mostly chose the books; the activity was given high status through parental involvement and teacher enthusiasm. Children nominated favourites and often went back to that book. Andrew, a sixth-year pupil whose uncle worked in the Royal Household, had alighted on a book about the royal family. He talked for some time about his experiences of visiting parts of the royal grounds and exploring the carriages and the stables, whilst using the book to add to and confirm his knowledge. Dean, a second-year boy, was given a large picture dictionary for his birthday and brought it into school every day and gradually became more proficient at naming a number of the pictures. The public debate over 'real books' and reading scheme books misses the point (see Campbell 1992). Real books, we argue, are those through which children make connections with public knowledge, and they consequently perform a much wider role than just helping children to learn to read.

Secondly, books confirm pupils' knowledge gained about stories which were read and told to them when they were very young such as fairy stories. They develop their oral narrative skills during the early part of their lives and begin to use literate technology to think with, mainly when they go to school (Egan 1988). They therefore have some knowledge of the form in which books are produced, that is, their narrative form is gained from their experiences of their oral cultures. So their interest in books when they arrive in school might be seen for many children as a reconnection with a narrative form they know well. Children also use them as a resource for their imagination and new knowledge, but books, like oral traditions, also contain other features, as Laura remarked: 'I think literature is just so important in terms of carrying culture and knowledge, and you know what people have been doing all these thousands of years if not to build something up. This is a way of carrying it on and passing it on.'

Wendy talked earlier (see p. 85) about the collaboration involved in her children preparing scripts for a puppet show, and here she describes why she feels that it is important to re-present myths and legends in a school setting:

> We were doing stories that term and we looked at lots of different myths and fairy tales. I just think working with a story, a mythical story, is very good for them. Even though they're Year 6 children it is useful for them to get to know that story and work with it. It has been good for that group of four or five who would find story writing independently very difficult and for the children who are abler. They had to do a character sketch of their puppet. They had to draw it, they had to write down the character of the puppet before they even made it. There's some quite sophisticated work you can get out of it. Across the range of ability there's something in there for everybody in terms of the language. For a start, the understanding of story, the character, and then they all wrote their own part. They said what their character was going to say. So they're thinking about direct speech, and having a puppet there meant that the actual oral skills of speaking were used.

Thirdly, books offer opportunities to explore a wide range of language forms, such as poetry, rhyming stories, nonsense rhymes, playground songs, stories with repetitive phrases, a mix of adventure stories, books without text, picture dictionaries, colourful information books, old favourites and fairy stories, and pop-up and sliding masks stories. Thea also focuses on word puzzles and games:

> It's just getting them interested in books and again reading books to them. I've read an enormous amount of children's literature myself. I think that's important because if you're recommending a book to a child then you have to know what it's about, or if they're talking to you about it, so that children will really respond to you more if you know something that they know. I love word games and word puzzles, playing around with words, word loops and so on, which I find has always helped them to develop an interest in it, looking for patterns in words which help with their spellings.

The children in Marilyn's class particularly enjoyed a book devoted to pig jokes and had memorized many of them. They regaled visitors with the jokes and brought them to talk sessions on the carpet.

Fourthly, children use the narrative form to re-present their perspectives and experiences by creating their own books as symbols of personal knowledge, as Thea again outlines:

> Making books in the classroom I find very successful because the children get ownership of their own, they are the author, it's important to them. They feel so proud that they've accomplished something, that they know from having seen and heard authors, that it takes them a long time to write, to get into print, that they have actually managed to accomplish that themselves. In fact when Jill Murphy [a children's author] came in, all the children were putting their hands up in my class saying 'We've done books, we can show ours to you'. That's identification with a writer, saying we're writers as well, knowing that there was a similarity there.

Thus Emma and her Year 2 friends decided to write the report of their visit to the Science Museum in the form of a book. They got their own equipment – scissors, glue, paper, colouring pencils – wrote up their report, constructed titles, designed the cover page, and described themselves as authors. They discussed each others' designs, and some changes were made to their books in the process. In another instance in Laura's class, Natalie and two friends decided during a 'choice' session to construct a book based on the 'Not Now Bernard' story. In their book the central character became themselves and their family, and the descriptions related to their own homes and experiences.

In Wendy's fifth-year class, the production of books is more formalized:

> I think they really get a lot out of that, they really do. When you look around sometimes they are really very involved in reading each other's stories and I prefer them to write a really long story. I find

they really get involved with their characters, they really enjoy their stories. A lot of the language work comes from the drafting. There's three lots of drafting. There's one on their own, one with the sub-editor, one with me . . . I find they're really proud. Last time, we made hardback books, with their own spines and we sewed all the pages in. This term I won't do that. I'll put a card cover on to a small exercise book because we're doing other things. But it's nice we always put a card cover on and put an illustrated picture on the front, think about the layout of the lettering and tacky-back it so they've got a book to take home and show their family.

Fifthly, books are used to generate interest in issues. Books are often se-lected because of the problems or dilemmas posed in the narratives. This is in line with Egan's (1988) recommendation to approach the curriculum in terms of binary opposites, so children can explore situations and contexts in problematic terms. Marilyn, whom we observed reading books con-cerned with Sarajevo and English travellers, also read a story about Columbus's voyage from the perspective of a child on Columbus's ship. She and the pupils discussed the life on board and the way the Spaniards treated the Indians: 'So we were trying to give them the South American Indians' perspective on it as you would do in any situation, try and sort out whose opinion do we listen to. Do we listen to the opinion of the Indians, the sailors, Columbus? What's the difference? Who's right? If you were Spanish, who would be right?'

Laura used a story book called *The Bird That Flew Beyond Time* which personalizes the Earth and tells a story about how it came near to death, as part of her world topic. She then asked the children to explain some of the phrases:

I wonder what's wrong with the Earth? . . . What do you think it means here when the Earth is saying 'my great seas and rivers are filled with poisonous waste which hurt the beaches'? . . . Right, why do you think people have to put rubbish in the sea then, Kayla? . . . There's another part where it says 'my tall forests are dying or being cut down so I can no longer breathe properly'. Put your hand up if you're going to tell me something about that . . . There's another thing here that puzzles me a little bit and I don't know if anybody can understand what this means. Stephanie, perhaps you'll be able to tell us. It's where it says 'the clouds that are fed with moisture from my forest no longer gather and rain cannot fall from them'. What does that mean? Really, really difficult this bit. It says 'my sky is torn and the sun's burning rays injure me'. The sun can be too hot. What does it mean, do you think, 'my sky is torn'? That's the bit I find very difficult . . . Right, Rosa says all the petrol from cars is going up in the sky and it makes the sky really horrible, and we breathe it in. Can it make the sky be torn? I wonder, I think it's something we're going to have to think about.

Laura uses a fictionalized story to address environmental issues, allows the children to use imagination, speculation and public knowledge as well as using shared puzzlement to establish 'common knowledge' (see Chapter 7).

Sixthly, the use of books encourages a critical approach. Our teachers were concerned to ensure that pupils articulated their opinions, attitudes and feelings. Book reviews, both oral and written, were a regular feature of the classroom. Laura occasionally asked the children to justify their selection of a book to take home. Her aims were:

> To develop children who enjoy reading or are readers who continue to read even after they've left school and don't have to. Who don't just read books like Jeffrey Archer, they read all sorts of books by all sorts of different people and they're able to be critical about them. Children who don't just read the clichés that are put about by the popular tabloids. They actually read through an article and find out as much as possible of what's really happening. Maybe look at two different sorts of papers and think, 'What does this really mean? What are these people really saying?' People being really critical but not destructive. I suppose the major way is asking them to look at literature and saying what they think about it and what's good about things, and not accepting it when they say 'but it was nice because it was funny'. And always going back to them and saying, 'Why do you find it nice? Why do you find it funny?' – getting them to have an opinion, and to feel that they've got the right to have an opinion.

She is also sure that having an opinion as a teacher is important in encouraging children to have opinions: 'We can't afford to have teachers, particularly at the primary range, that aren't themselves able to discuss literature, that aren't themselves able to pick up one of those children's books and tell their class why they enjoy it or why they don't enjoy it or what they think is good about it.'

Seventhly, books are important for encouraging an affective response. In Chapter 4 we showed the importance of the emotions in a primary pedagogy, and how affective experiences are bound up with cognitive. Egan (1988) argues that the affective is neglected in modern education, but can be reinstated by use of the story. He notes that stories are mainly about how people feel, and that this is important for full understanding. Also, the fact that stories have an ending invest them with affective power. He claims 'What is completed by the ending of a good story is the pattern that fixes the meaning and our feelings about the contents' (p. 31).

In this vein, Marilyn generated a considerable number of book reviews during our research period which were discussed, analysed and critiqued by the Year 6 pupils themselves. In some of the reviews, the pupils referred to the emotional impact of the stories. Catrina reviewed the *Nine Lives of Montezuma* by Michael Morpurgo and wrote: 'It was a good and exciting book to read. Every life the cat had, it died. This can leave you feeling many different emotions.' John wrote about his feelings while reading *Little Foxes* by the same author: 'Billy Bunch found a wilderness and the animals he finds there give him a new life and when his secret place is discovered and the last fox is threatened by hunters, Billy doesn't hesitate to join in its flight. When I was reading the book I thought I would like to be Billy Bunch.'

Hayley wrote a review of *The Island of Strangers* by Catherine Sefton. In the book two girls from different backgrounds, one urban, the other a rural traveller, clash:

> Nora and Crystal hate each other, but then all of a sudden they are sort of friends. The relationship between Nora and Crystal is the most interesting in the book. I think that Nora and Crystal are scared of each other really, but they just don't want to show it so they act tough towards each other. I really think you should read this book because it is really adventurous and exciting. The book is about relationships and it really makes you think deep down.

Marilyn, is very keen to use stories to address personal feelings:

> I'm very aware of using stories to address whatever's going on in their lives. I know that I did at the beginning of this year. We had a term talking about literacy in our staff meetings and INSET, and in talking about it I was amazed that when I was talking about books and talking about stories, addressing issues, that there were teachers who don't see that as part of the book culture thing. They don't seem to realize that stories reflect their [children's] experiences and that they should build on their experiences. They didn't seem to realize that stories teach. There are teachers who see books merely as a tool for teaching reading. Reading is not about print on the page, it's not about that at all.

Apple (1993: 49) has argued that texts are political documents:

> They signify, through their content and form, particular constructs of reality, particular ways of selecting and organizing that vast universe of possible knowledge. They embody . . . someone's selection, someone's vision of legitimate knowledge and culture, one that in the process of enfranchising one group's cultural capital disenfranchises another.

He notices, however, that there is always 'space for more democratic action', and 'openings for counter-hegemonic activity' (p. 10). We would argue that our teachers are trying to create space for children 'for demo-cratic action'. Through encouraging them to exercise choice, engage in criticism, establish ownership of knowledge and make connections with their own cultures, interrogate texts, and relate them to social and polit-ical issues, teachers are encouraging children to construct their own dis-course and their own knowledge.

TALK

While books and private study are important modes of engaging with narrative and story, by far the most important is talk. Teachers encour-aged dialogue and comment, and occasionally intervened with higher-order questions. In some classes the atmosphere was less formal and the teacher's voice would often rise just above the children's hum to make a point, ask a question, pose a problem or to note a child's piece of work. Gradually, the hum would die down if she wished to continue for any length and she wanted to involve the class as a whole. Turn taking was an essential component of organization of dialogue, but the teachers sometimes let more of a general hubbub continue. On occasions, this was to encourage children to react intuitively to each other's comments and partly to organize their own interchanges. At other times, it seemed the teachers were waiting for what they considered an interesting story or observation, which they would seize on to develop, perhaps, an idea or an issue, or to enhance a particular child's esteem. This mostly hap-pened in more formal class sessions, where the teacher would sometimes listen for a few minutes to a number of children commenting or argu-ing, and then gently talk over the children's comments to draw out a rel-evant contribution, or to make a relevant observation, or to gain silence in order to listen to one child. Teachers also often summarized contri-butions, partly for clarification, partly to develop the discussion. Certainly teachers had enormous power to influence the direction of the inter-changes (Baker and Perrott 1988), but by creating an atmosphere where talk is almost endemic they are ensuring a more effective development of 'common knowledge'. The effectiveness of dialogue and discussion for learning is supported elsewhere (for example, Gipps 1992; Bruner 1972; McLean 1992).

Edwards and Mercer (1987) assert that knowledge and thought are not just to do with how people think but are intrinsically social and cultural. They therefore look at how 'common knowledge' is constructed through joint activity and discourse. They argue that the things that are said are only the tip of an iceberg, and that the great hidden mass beneath is essential to the nature of what is openly visible. They go on to propose that:

By looking at learning from a theoretical perspective which does not assume the overriding supremacy of action over talk, or which defines learning purely in terms of individual cognitions, one gains new insights into the social, cultural, and communicative basis of human cognition and learning. These insights – into how adults structure children's learning, how children interpret terms, tasks and activities, how teachers and pupils succeed or fail in establishing a mutuality, a shared universe of discourse – are valuable in themselves.

(p. 168)

Tireless talk

The dominance of teacher talk in classrooms has often been presented in the form of critique of the pedagogy involved (Flanders 1970; Delamont 1976). However, teaching effectiveness depends on the kind and quality of talk. In our classrooms, 'tireless talk' plays a central role in creating the 'shared universe of discourse' that Edwards and Mercer (1987: 168) argue is so important to the creation of 'common knowledge'. It is a form of teacher talk that is constant, and generally positive and thoughtful. It can be comforting, challenging, imaginative and enthusiastic. Tireless talk has a number of contexts – whole-class situations involving both formal carpet sessions and short pauses during activities, groups and talk with individuals. It also involves a range of content, from organization of activities, transmitting information, exhibiting examples of valued work to the sharing and development of cognitive and affective processes. Three distinctive effects that we noted were: inspiring confidence among pupils, developing dialogue, and making connections with public knowledge.

Inspiring confidence

Far from being intrusive or dominating, 'tireless talk' creates a relaxed atmosphere which reduces fear and apprehension and encourages pupil contributions. The welcome session in the morning is full of a variety of conversations between teachers and pupils and between pupils themselves, for example, Grace providing humorous excuses for a child's lateness (having first ascertained the reason), Theresa cracking jokes about outing money being lost in her washing machine, and Marilyn discussing with some girls their swimming session the previous evening. Early discussions about activities were punctuated with questions from the children concerning organization. After they had settled into activities the teacher's voice could be heard rising slightly above the children's voices as she praised some work or made a joke. During the day, the whole class was stopped from time to time to examine a problem – what might come next in a food chain, or which planet is nearer the sun, or how to seal the leak in a water candle. The children were involved in dealing with people who came into the room with requests for information, and they were kept informed of daily school events such as classes on school trips and the arrival of visitors.

By contrast, silences were often full of tension. Sometimes this might be for purposes of control. Teachers used long pauses, deliberate and slow, articulated phrases and low voices to quieten a class or admonish a particular pupil. On other occasions, creating such a tension may be part of the teacher's pedagogy, for example, telling stories, or generating interest, as Theresa did when she described some aspects of Elizabethan life (see Chapter 5).

Developing dialogue

In a conversation with a group of Year 2 children concerning their designs for their dance drama characters and costumes, the teacher's interjections were constructed to extend ('What colours would they be?'), to encourage ('Black and green, that's great!'), to ensure continuity ('So that would be a ... ?'), to focus the discussion ('The thing that interests me a little bit ... was the poem was about the magic eggs ...'), to stimulate ('They could be magic creatures'), to clarify ('Aren't they eggs?'), and to lighten the discourse by providing humour ('The ideas are really hatching now, aren't they?'). Having got the ideas whizzing, the teacher concluded the interchange with 'I would like you to go and do some work on that'. In this conversation the Year 2 children contributed freely and used each other's ideas to develop their own as Natalie, one of the children, shows here when she suggested a beginning for the dance drama. She talked very excitedly:

> Laura, I've got a brilliant idea. Somebody could quickly put the egg in the middle when everyone could look round and pretend they don't know what it is, and one of us could be a bird. One of us could go inside the egg and we could curl up in it and all the other creatures could move the egg around. One of us could be inside and we could move the egg around and they could start peeling the egg off and then they see this little bird or butterfly come out.

Pupils were given the chance to comment to themselves, to each other, repeat what was being said in their own way, engage in a response, call out, or add information to the point being made. Children's intuitive responses – the best approach to new knowledge or unfamiliar problems, according to Bruner (1986) – in the classes observed were not ignored. Such comments were often taken up by the teacher by either passing them on for others to consider or by getting the child to explain the relevance with some 'empathetic challenging' (Bonnett 1991).

Making connections with public knowledge

Teachers exploit children's familiarity with a narrative form to make connections with public knowledge. When discussing a science activity to bleach some tights for the dance drama, Laura allowed a narrative to take place concerning the use of bleach in swimming pools. The children had nearly all been swimming and this diversion appeared to substantiate the conceptualization of bleach as a special chemical. These apparent diversions appeared to be part of a more natural discourse and therefore assisted in making connections with public knowledge. On another occasion the researcher brought a large melon in for the children for assisting him with the research. Laura spent some time talking to the children about how to divide it equally and then asked the class to decide which fruit could represent the planets in order of size, as this was their current topic. It was decided that the strawberry could be Pluto and the melon Jupiter. In the following example, Laura is explaining to her class about how to do a mathematical transposition exercise involving a giant. The children had to make the giant twice the size of the example by redrawing it on a grid twice the size of the original. After she had explained the task and partly drawn her transposition, she suggested that they humanized her giant by giving it a character and an environment. She used their topic theme of space and the planets to do this. As she talks to them she is gradually colouring her giant and adding relevant detail:

Laura: The important thing is that life gets a bit boring. Well,
            I'll tell you something about my giant. This is my giant.
            He actually doesn't live on this planet, he lives on a
            different planet. He lives on a planet that's very, very
            close to the sun. It's closer to the sun than our planet
            and it's got a very red sky. That's probably because it's so
            close to the sun, and it has big swirly, yellow clouds
            around it. Do you know what that planet's called? What
            do you think it's called, Theresa?
Theresa: Jupiter.
Laura: It's not Jupiter, Jupiter's farther away from the sun. This
            is a planet that is very close to the sun. It goes very
            quickly round the sun, very speedy planet, what do you
            think, Kayla?
Kayla: Mars.
Laura: Not Mars, you've got the first letter right, it begins with
            an M, what do you think, Junior?
Junior: Mercury.
Laura: Yes, it's the planet Mercury. This giant lives on the planet
            Mercury very close to the sun. Of course scientists think
            that nothing can live on the planet because it's so hot
            and dried up but there's great yellow clouds round it.
            They are clouds that would be poisonous to us but
            because of this my giant has got a bright red face and

his face has got greeny spots on it from all the poison clouds. So, his skin's like that as well and it's because he lives on this very hot planet with poisonous clouds.

Laura herself mixes some facts about Mercury with her imagination concerning the giant's susceptibility to poisonous clouds, but she uses opportunities set up by the children to confirm other scientific aspects related to oxygen.

Kayleigh: What if we landed on there with a rocket and we didn't get out?
Laura: We'd have to have a special rocket ship and special clothes to protect us from the hot sun. It's very, very hot and there's not enough oxygen so we would need oxygen to breathe.
Kayleigh: Yes, we'd have that oxygen thing.
Laura: Yes, we'd have to take oxygen with us. You're right. OK now I'm a bit worried about his hair actually. His hair has got a bit stiff because he's in this very, very hot place. Ever so curly, it's curlier than the curliest hair you have ever seen because it's so hot, and his hair is actually quite a dark green colour. Ever so, ever so curly and he actually protects his hair by wearing an enormous hat and of course, you can only draw these extras in when you've finished the whole giant and you're through. Also, because he has to walk on this very, very hot planet my giant wears very special boots. They're purple and red boots. They're made of a very special material to stop his feet getting too hot. Now that's my giant. Your giant might be different, it might live in all sorts of strange places. He might live up a mountain where it's very cold.

She now encourages them to use their imagination tempered with the necessity to deal with environmental conditions.

Ashley: Like, you know that story about thunder . . .
Laura: Right, so, your giant is going to look . . .
Kayleigh: Like a unicorn.
Laura: Kayleigh is going to put a horn on her giant so he can be a unicorn giant. Right, you could have the giant who maybe lives under the earth. What would that sort of giant look like? Just think what sort of, what his skin might look like. Right, well, you've got to decide. What do you think, Shareen?
Shareen: It would be all brown.
Laura: Right, where would your giant live, what sort of place?

Shareen:	Up in the mountains.
Laura:	Up in the mountains. Would he live in a mountain where it's quite hot or a mountain where it's very cold?
Shareen:	Where it's very cold.
Laura:	Where it's very cold. OK, so what sort of clothes would he have on?
Shareen:	He would have on all winter clothes.
Laura:	Winter clothes to keep him . . . ?
Shareen:	Warm.
Laura:	Warm, OK. I wonder what colours those clothes might be. Some people on mountains wear very bright clothes so they show up, so people can find them easily, and sometimes people wear clothes that are the same colour as the places where they live so people can't find them. You have to decide about your giant. What sort of person is your giant, does he want to be found, does he want to show up or does he want to hide so that people can't find him?
Shareen:	He wants to show up.
Laura:	Yours wants to show up does he? OK well, I want you to think about what your giant is like. There's all sorts of planets he could come from. He could come from Mercury, like my giant. He could come from Venus. Now Venus is rather a beautiful planet, in fact, Venus has yellow clouds around it as well. He could come from all sorts of different places on planet Earth.
David:	It could be a planet in a mountain.
Laura:	Planet in a mountain, that's an amazing idea.

Cleverly, she gains their interest in the exercise through using narrative, and then brings in knowledge about specific features of planets in a context where talk is the key to the development. Laura commented,

> They [the children] can't take on board the enormity of the whole idea of the universe and the distances, and the fact that it could take all your life to go from one planet to another because it's so mind boggling. But if you talk to them about it and you do quite a lot of imagining, or what would it be like if . . . , then the things start coming through. They're putting ideas together. They're putting thoughts together. Isn't it interesting how much there is in their heads, the ideas.

Time for talk

We have noted, in Chapter 3, the time pressures imposed on teachers by the National Curriculum. However, time is an essential prerequisite for talk and the development of narrative, and these teachers created time for this talk. This was substantiated by the cursory survey of how time was spent in three classrooms over a three-day period in each of them. As well as collecting rudimentary statistics on reading times, we collected statistics on carpet times or class times. Some of this carpet time was taken up with reading and administration and that has been counted in those particular categories. The time taken up by talk-related activities not concerned with reading and administration and connected to narratives and curriculum examination varied from 20 to 25 per cent of classroom time. When faced with these statistics none of the teachers was surprised or concerned about the amount of time spent together as a class. Marilyn describes her role and justifies the use of the time:

I'm trying to think of the sessions that we had in those three days [when researchers were there]. There was that huge one on anti-racism. That was the one which, as we said at the time, wasn't planned to go on that long. If they [class sessions] are not just the basic, 'Right sit down, this is what you're going to do now, this group go here', organizational, management-type stuff, I would say it would normally start with some teaching points from me which then goes into discussion, and I try not to be the dominant voice in the discussion. I like to answer questions that they put and I get cross if the children interrupt the answer when the child is asked something I want to know. There's a lot of social instruction going on into holding conversations, group conversations . . . I can remember as an infant teacher the things that kids bring in from home [were important] as well. There was always an awful lot of talk with infants about what they did at home, what did you do at the weekend, what have you been doing, what did you do last night. I can remember the point where, when we first began with the National Curriculum, suddenly we were feeling under pressure about it. We did these exercises in wasted time. We did things like stopping taking the register, because it was 'evaporated time', this magic evaporated time and people started to think 'Oh, we can't do that, haven't got time for that'. I can remember the discussions going on, not just in our school but also when you went to the Professional Development Centre. There would be people saying 'Can't do that any more can we, we haven't got time for that'. Gradually, people, certainly myself, realized that class time is far too valuable to let it go by the board. You can't stop doing that, it is such a fundamental part. OK, you can stick it in your speaking and listening part of the National Curriculum – and there's an awful lot of that goes on. But you can't take it away. It doesn't matter where they try to put the weighting in the new part of the history, for example, you can't take that part away unless we go back to sitting in rows and listening to the teacher and not participating at all.

Laura felt just as strongly, and she claimed that it is imaginative time that is being lost:

> Children's thinking grows from talk. As their imagination is allowed to roam, talking and real conversation feeds their imagination, particularly with adults to structure it a little bit, to just nurture it a little bit. I don't mean to direct it or to channel it too much, (rather) to just prompt here and there. I do think that we've got to develop conversational skills in children and put them in situations where they are going to have discussions and exchange ideas, and I just don't think this happens now. It doesn't happen for all sorts of reasons. The main one is because the curriculum is so totally overloaded that there's no way you get through the day without thinking 'Is this all I've done? I haven't ticked off enough today'.

Time for talk is essential for these teachers, not only because it is a strategy for covering the overload systematically by reducing the need for each child to have to do everything individually, but also because it is the medium for thought whereby children and adults develop their intellect and understanding.

CONCLUSION

Lyotard (1984) notes that, following the decline of meta-narratives, such as Marxism, there has been a shift of emphasis towards individualism. Although much of his writing celebrates the conception of a world in which the individual and the micro dominate, he is paradoxically concerned that in a fragmented individualistic society, with science dominating, narrative is also disappearing and so therefore the flexibility of a narrative knowledge in which the aesthetic, cognitive and moral are interwoven will also disappear. Why should this be relevant to the atmosphere of creative primary classrooms? The implementation of the National Curriculum is largely conceptualized as a matter of delivery to individual children. However, the attainment targets[1] do have the potential to be achieved through 'relationship-centred' education (Bonnett 1991).

Central to the future of this kind of education, according to Bonnett, are two crucial questions. Firstly, whether teachers believe sufficiently enough in its value to make opportunities to pursue it seriously, and whether they will receive the necessary help in terms of encouragement, time and resources to support them in the attempt (Bonnett 1991: 291). Bonnett argues that:

> the National Curriculum is not inherently hostile to the relationship-centred principle. . . . but that the cumulative requirements of plan-

ning, teaching, monitoring, and reporting such an extensive and detailed set of objectives as comprise the National Curriculum will pre-occupy teachers to such an extent that there is real danger of the concerns of children simply disappearing from view.

(p. 291)

These teachers have thought it still relevant and possible to pursue relationship education through social narrative forms. They recognize the significance of this form for the development of pupils in general, and also, perhaps, see the significance of this form countering the rational-calculative mode's exclusive claim to validity.

Secondly, a particular criticism of Lyotard's perspective concerning the nature of social development is that it celebrates little narratives (those of individuals) and condemns big narratives (those of social groups). What is significant about these teachers' practice in relation to narrative is that they highlight it as a form for learning and interpretation, and also organize *social* investigations of narratives. Further, they contextualize these situations in historical issues around gender, race, class and other social categories. In creating atmospheres where social narratives are highly legitimated, and in contextualizing a significant part of that process in historical and political issues, these teachers are resisting the moves towards little narratives, and are attempting to maintain a connection between micro experiences of the classroom and the macro influences of wider society.

NOTE

1 Attainment targets are 'the knowledge, skills and understanding which pupils of different abilities and maturities are expected to have reached by the end of each Key Stage' (Education Reform Act 1988), that is, at ages 7, 11, 14 and 16.

7

MANAGING THE CURRICULUM

There is overwhelming evidence to show that the National Curriculum in its first manifestation (1988–93) was clearly unmanageable (see, for example, Campbell and Neill 1994). But teachers had to get by somehow. How, then, did our teachers manage? The general problem lay in meeting legal requirements to deliver the National Curriculum while remaining true to their own values and beliefs where they differed. In practice, this broke down into a number of issues – making knowledge relevant; maintaining a holistic curriculum; sustaining a positive pupil identity; providing a focus on the process, as contrasted with the ends, of learning; and providing breadth of learning as well as depth. We consider each in turn.

RELEVANT KNOWLEDGE

The teachers placed a high priority on knowledge being meaningful to the child within the child's frame of reference, and thus becoming what we might term 'personal knowledge'. The National Curriculum contains a great deal of 'public knowledge', already existing and generally available, external to individuals. Given the unmanageability of the task, the easiest solution for teachers would be the totally pragmatic, but rather unprincipled, one of settling for a transmission form of teaching. Our teachers, however, were not willing to resort to a totally pragmatic response, though there was inevitably an element of that, as indeed there was before the National Curriculum (Berlak and Berlak 1981). How, then, did they at times manage to turn public into personal knowledge? We identified a number of strategies.

Sharing and creating knowledge
This strategy is used particularly with the class as a whole, where different children's perspectives add to the development of an idea or technique.

Children can adapt and modify their perspectives as they go along, taking control and ownership of a later activity through collective debate and argument, as when Marilyn asked a boy (Year 6) to show the class how he had constructed his model and what problems he had in doing so. Children's opinions and understandings were given prominence as 'experts' (Corno 1989) 'How would you tackle this? What kind of problems did you have and how did you solve them? Which would you select to do first? How do you know this is correct?' Thus, a spelling lesson ended with pupils explaining to others how they learnt their words and a number of different strategies were discussed. This shared collective knowledge was used to benefit all of them. A cooking activity where the children initially were not allowed to ask adults for help was constructed by Laura. The control was theirs within the boundaries of the task, and the knowledge generated was negotiated and shared with each other. As the session developed the children were stopped from time to time and asked to identify any problems. These were then discussed by the cooking groups or the whole class. Similarly, photographs of some children from Laura's class examining frogs and frog spawn were displayed on sheets of paper, and children were asked to say what they thought the children in the photos were saying or thinking (this was suggested by one of the pupils).

Spontaneous contributions were followed up by the group. Laura's children made a giant relating to a maths investigation on ratio. When the giant was found to be twice the length, it was suggested by a child during discussion that the giant might have kitchen utensils twice the size. So, two containers and a plate with cutlery were constructed by doubling the linear proportions of classroom utensils. The capacity of the giant's containers were then investigated and found to be eight times as large. In these examples, the teachers share the process of education with the learner (Bruner 1972) to develop 'problem finding'. This is extended further in the development of 'possibility knowledge'.

Possibility knowledge

As noted earlier, these teachers used imagination regularly in their conversations with children over the investigation of public knowledge, and as an end in itself. This yielded a form of 'possibility knowledge'. Children were encouraged to speculate about phenomena. Their constructions were played with by their peers and the teacher, and no firm conclusions were necessarily insisted upon. The teachers in these class sessions always encouraged children to contribute their speculations and knowledge; none of it was discounted by the teacher as invalid. The whole group would then be asked if they had alternative speculations or information to add, or if they wished to comment on the validity of individual contributions. The Year 2 children who discussed the story about the Earth being 'upset' at the level of pollution it was enduring had to discuss later the relevance of trees, oxygen and rain to their fantasy worlds that they had constructed out of boxes and junk.

Possibilities were encouraged in terms of issues, as we saw in the last chapter: for example, is the tooth fairy real? How does she carry the money? Why do racists behave the way they do? Why do we need trees? Is everything you see on television true? What can you tell about the person in this portrait? During some discussions during the cooking session some 'possibility knowledge' was considered, as this field note indicates:

> Whilst evaluating the cooking session involving coconut cakes, the children are faced with the question of where the water went. After 'eliciting' the term 'evaporation' from Kayla, a 7-year-old child, Laura presses her as to what this means. Kayla suggests it goes to make clouds, and Laura asks whether there are coconut clouds up there. Kayla leaps on to this idea and confirms Laura's humorous suggestions by talking about how she has experienced being under a coconut cloud drinking up all the coconut. Without rationalizing this idea, Laura moves the group on to talk about the problems they had with the exercise.

These examples, together with others mentioned in earlier chapters, such as the discussion about the giant and the kind of planet on which it lived, and Grace's discussion with her children about life in St Lucia, show how the teachers mix personal knowledge, imaginative knowledge and speculation to construct their perspectives of the world. Imagination in this sense is not a tool or a concept to illuminate knowledge but an essential component of it.

Prior knowledge

In early years' educational thinking it is generally recognized that new understandings can only be based on pupils' prior knowledge (Siraj-Blatchford 1993). Interest in an activity or task is also closely related to prior knowledge of the phenomena (Tobias 1994). Prior knowledge often derives from home, or from children's background culture, giving substance to the concept of 'bringing home' knowledge that might otherwise be alienated (Berger and Luckmann 1967). In introducing new areas for investigation the teachers nearly always started with what the children knew already and accepted speculation and fantasies. These were then examined by the group as a whole and, if appropriate, tasks resulted from the questions that arose. For example, the school pond was full of frogs, and Laura asked what the children knew about them. There was a dispute about sexing frogs and some children were sent away to use reference books to establish the characteristics of a frog's sex. The teacher made use of the child's personal knowledge.

On occasions when the teacher used public knowledge as a starting point, the children would be asked to indicate what they already knew about the subject and what opinions they held. The theory is that public knowledge gains status in the pupils' eyes through the status given to children's knowledge in the first place and the connection made by the teacher between the two. The teacher enhances the child's ownership of any knowledge and brings new knowledge into the classroom for investigation and appropriation by the children. The investigation of the phenomena includes counterperspectives, which are incorporated within comfortable low-risk situations. For example, knowledge of the life cycle of a human embryo, investigated by Marilyn's class (Year 6) was situated in valuing their knowledge first, and then by building on their interest developed through personal connections and experiences of family life.

Shared puzzlement

This strategy affects children's perception of the differential power relations between the teacher as a centre of knowledge and the children as receivers of knowledge. The teacher puts herself in the same personal position as the child. They look out at the world together and surmise about the future of the world, or why linear measurements are not in the same ratio as measurements of capacity. Shared puzzlement leads to shared solutions – a joint construction of knowledge:

> Laura and the children are bleaching some tights for their costumes for their dance drama and they are not clear why they won't turn white. This puzzlement is shared and left unsolved in the short term, though suggestions are made by the group as to how they might find out why, such as contacting the manufacturers. The mystery as to why the volume of the giant's containers should be a different ratio from the linear measurement is explored together, as the teacher allows herself to be part of the 'shared knowledge' being developed by the group based on discourse and joint action. She expresses her non-understanding, and ways of addressing the problem are discussed as a group.

The National Curriculum has a 'realist' approach to knowledge (Burwood 1992), making a virtue out of public knowledge, denying the social construction of knowledge and selecting the knowledge to be addressed. Our teachers, however, are concerned that a variety of knowledges are legitimated and valued, and that the nature of knowledge in political and power terms is confronted by their pupils.

Valuing pupil knowledge

Just as teachers in the Education Reform Act of 1988 are regarded as technicians, deliverers of a curriculum, so pupils are regarded as clients, receivers of it. This is a view of the pupil circumscribed by the bounded world of the National Curriculum and national assessment. Our teachers have a different view of the pupils, a more holistic one that sees them as persons, to whom school is but one situation and experience in their lives. What happens outside school is critical for what happens within it – it is all of a piece. To our teachers, to section off school experience in the notion of pupil as client is not only depriving them of genuine educational opportunities, but depriving them of their full status as persons. The teachers tackled this problem in various ways.

Pupil knowledge in terms of experience needs to be valued, not just because it helps legitimize public knowledge, but because it supports the positive feelings pupils have about themselves. Thus, Andrew's (Year 6) knowledge of the royal family, mentioned earlier in Chapter 6 gained through an uncle who works in the Royal Household, was supported by Marilyn, his teacher. Books were provided by the teacher so pupils could reinforce the status of their knowledge, and they were encouraged to express and evaluate their knowledge. Children's cultural backgrounds were also used as a resource and a way of confirming their identity. Thus a Chinese cultural day was acknowledged by the teacher, and Ning, a Year 2 pupil, told the class about the rituals involved. It might be noted that using personal or cultural knowledge to boost self-esteem also assists in the process of learning *about* knowledge, in that knowledge has perspectives, values and beliefs embedded in it.

Pupils gain self-esteem in terms of what they know and can tell, and how the articulation of that knowledge is received by teachers and peers. Ian (Year 6) took great pleasure in showing the researcher and other people around an exhibition of the class models and display constructed after a school journey which included a visit to Corfe castle. He told tales and passed on information about the Civil War with some relish and enjoyment. As mentioned earlier, interest in a topic together with prior knowledge is seen as productive for a basis for further in-depth investigations (Tobias 1994). Encouraging an interest is seen as a priority, as opposed to attempting to convey substantial chunks of knowledge about a particular topic. This may partly account for the popularity of maths in most of the classes including Marilyn's: 'You just get into it', 'I like finishing it', 'I like getting more done', 'I'm relieved to get it done and upset that I can't do any more'. When asked how they would help other pupils with maths, they reflected their teachers' methods in terms of supportive assistance. Andrew, of the Royal Household interest, said:

> I'd get a scrap of paper and write it down and point out the child's mistakes and show them the way. And make them change it...I wouldn't give them the answer (*laughingly*). I wouldn't have a go at them if they got it wrong, because they're trying to learn. It's not their fault if they try and they put their mind to it and they couldn't get the answer.

Developing 'common knowledge'

As discussed earlier, 'common knowledge' is developed by teacher and pupil in order that the teacher can assist the student across the zone of proximal development (Edwards and Mercer 1987). This 'common knowledge' is not only cognitive knowledge. Some common knowledge is developed between pupils and teachers that relates directly to the pupil's identity, such as facing challenges, managing social relations, co-operation and methods of decision-making. During the anti-racist discussion, Georgina challenged a friendly suggestion from a white pupil that one of the black children should read a poem written by a Jamaican poet. She asked why it had to be a black child. Georgina's view of her teacher's reaction, gained in a later conversation, was that Marilyn accepted challenges, always remained calm and allowed everyone to have their say, unlike many other teachers who would decide, sometimes angrily, what was permissible and what was not. A group of children from the same class also noticed how Marilyn handled disputes and disagreements in the class and told us that this approach had had a positive effect on their collaboration and behaviour towards each other. The children were encouraged to choreograph part of their musical and were given time alone to work it out together, and they dealt with disagreements by using models that they had seen Marilyn use. The whole class were involved in deciding who should play the parts in the musical by being encouraged to say who they thought would best fit each part. The common knowledge is also developed in the process of investigation. These teachers worked at pupils' tables with groups, e.g. making sand timers and constructing bingo games for multiplication tables. Whilst the teachers were developing cognitive skills, through the open and challenging questions they constantly used they also shared common knowledge related to approach and collective investigation. Such techniques are important to working-class children (as noted earlier in Chapter 5) and, from pupil's comments, seem to be very productive.

Problematizing knowledge

These teachers believe that there is a direct connection between the development of the individual in holistic terms and the 'secondary socialization' carried out by educational institutions, explained in Chapter 4, that of connecting the child who has come from an intense identity process with parents to the more generalized institutions of society (Berger and Luckman 1967). We have argued, in Chapter 4, that primary teachers recognize this distinction and attempt to bring home the established knowledge through affective connections. In this way, the primary school could be seen as a mixture of both primary and secondary socialization.

However, recently a new perspective has refocused the notion of power from how it represses to how it is deployed, that is, to the ways in which power works its way through the social body to produce social practices and identity. Foucault (1970) argues that we should reverse the traditional belief that knowledge is power, and define power as embodied in the manner by which people gain knowledge and use it to intervene in their social affairs. This seems to relate to creative teaching, in that we have observed not only multiple conditions of knowledge and experiential learning, but atmospheres of critique and emotion which affect the manner of engagement with knowledge. This is illustrated by a sharing of ideas between pupils about how to learn spellings, and the making of connections between fantasy and mathematical transformations and ratio through the construction of a giant and explorations of a world it inhabits (see pp. 110–12).

This view of power and knowledge also opens up the question of what kind of knowledge people are gaining. With our teachers, it would appear that it may be a knowledge of 'self' as representative of the culture. In problematizing knowledge, as some of our teachers did at times, they were possibly problematizing the identity of the pupil. Thus, Laura, the Year 2 teacher, investigating 'worlds', encouraged children to redesign models and costumes at any time during the six weeks of the topic, which included a gradual introduction of new techniques and perspectives. This was enhanced by investigations of pollution and environmental issues, as we have seen, which illuminated the power relations involved in public knowledge. In this learning process the children were encouraged to 'play' with their own perspectives, reflect and discuss other perspectives, and the concept of power relations was used to consider aspects of the scientific perspective of our world. This approach not only related directly to the nature of knowledge but also to appreciation of each child's separate identity within the collective framework of the classroom.

MAINTAINING A HOLISTIC CURRICULUM

The decision to construct a National Curriculum around subjects, instead of, for example, 'areas of learning and experience' (DES 1985), or a set of values (White 1993), is having far-reaching effects on teachers who have been used to a more cross-curricular approach. Strong classification (Bernstein 1971) constructs distinct boundaries around subjects and insulates them both from each other, and from the teacher, reducing the power of the teacher over what they transmit. True, the prescription included some cross-curricular provision in the form, mainly, of five themes; and the National Curriculum Council appeared to attempt to reinstate the 'whole curriculum' by emphasizing cross-curricular strategies which would meld together the separate parts into an organic whole (NCC 1989); but Maw (1993: 72) argued that 'the model of the whole curriculum which results is inherently unstable because it attempts an equilibrium between conflicting models of curriculum construction'. The task of co-ordination was thus left to teachers. Hargreaves (1991: 39) feared that 'teachers will simply treat the advice on cross-curricular provision in a mechanical way, using checklists to demonstrate that the five themes are being dealt with.' However, there are some possibilities. Bolton (1993) notes that the law says nothing about how a subject is to be organized, nor insists that subjects should be taught separately, nor prescribes methods and materials. Bernstein (1975: 101) stipulates a number of conditions if an integrated curriculum were to be achieved, notably 'some relational idea, a supra-content concept, which focuses upon general principles at a high level of abstraction'. An example of a 'relational idea' operating at school level was noted in Woods (1995). As Chitty (1993: 85) points out, 'the term "whole curriculum" means different things to different schools; and the available evidence suggests . . . that school curriculum models are still more or less coherent according to a number of factors that have much to do with the individual philosophy of the schools themselves'.

It was apparent from talking to and observing our teachers that the issue of a holistic approach meant something to them. Many of the teachers worked to provide a holistic experience for the children around a linking theme, for they believed that this is natural and an appropriate way to encourage learning. Norma thought children learn best by networking with experiences:

> It's how anybody learns. You take a topic of any sort and it has spin-offs, children don't learn in a linear process. For example, a group of children and myself were joining hexagonals together and trying to establish a formula for the number needed to make the next step in a developing pattern. Some children had the bright idea of making it into a game. They used previous experience of an oracy project in which they had been involved where games played a large part. In National Curriculum terms they were using maths, geography and language. The process of learning, thinking and creating should come first and then assessment in National Curriculum terms. This form of 'network learning' is cross-curricular.

How does the philosophy operate at teacher level, given a favourable school situation? We noticed three particular strategies here: incorporation, a thematic approach and embodying the basics.

Incorporation

One of the favourite ways among primary teachers to integrate is through topics. The extent to which they have been used in a multidisciplinary sense in the past has often been exaggerated (Galton 1995). Regardless of this, they have come under attack, as if they permeate the whole of primary education. It seems that thematic or topic approaches are considered incompatible with the National Curriculum because they are integrally connected with the Plowdenesque ideology which central government has been anxious to discredit. Teachers have been urged, consequently, to do less of them, except where they are specifically promoting the National Curriculum, and to do more whole-class teaching (Alexander *et al.* 1992; National Curriculum Council 1993; OFSTED 1993).

Some, however, fear that much valuable practice would be lost (Woods 1993; Webb 1993; Dadds 1994). Webb (1993) shows that there has been a shift towards whole-class teaching amongst primary teachers, and a subject focus for topics appears to be becoming more frequent, though for pragmatic rather than principled reasons (OFSTED 1993; Webb 1993).

However, we did observe the incorporation of other subjects into a one-subject-centred topic (see also Woods and Wenham 1994; Woods 1995). For example, in a history topic, drama eventually became the main focus, with a musical being prepared and performed to parents which included children's contributions in terms of choreography and musical composition. The musical Marilyn's pupils performed about Tudor times is one way in which she promoted history. The pupils were asked throughout the project to evaluate their involvement. Debbie (Year 6) noted: 'What I hate about history is when you have to learn all the dates, and you can't do it. If history is done the way we did (through our drama and art), then I would chose it at secondary school.'

Theresa also used the topic of Tudors and Stuarts to draw out a number of mathematical skills in terms of area, scale and measurement through the construction of Tudor gardens in 2D but with 3D mustard and cress boundaries. Science was introduced by the children digging over the school garden and planting bulbs and flowers after stories of how Tudor explorers brought new plants back from South America. This was enhanced by geographical connections and close observational drawings were done to simulate the work of the explorers. Language and stories were also involved. Theresa brought into school specialist dancers who taught the children some Tudor dances which were performed by the children.

Later in the term the children constructed Elizabethan portraits and miniatures. This involved a specialist art teacher, an artist parent talking to the class about books she had illustrated, and a visit to the National Portrait Gallery which included a talk about deconstructing pictures. The children's report of their visit involved an emphasis on alternative presentations, and innovative design was encouraged. These portraits were accompanied by poetry based on flattering descriptions of Queen Elizabeth after investigation of the Queen's alopecia and smallpox scars which affected fashions of the court. How did Theresa assess this activity?:

If I assessed it in practical terms, it was a pleasant idea, we got a pleasant end product and a pleasant end result. However, I would also expect the strength and depth of their work not necessarily to be the tactile end product of their work. It is the sort of seepage, the seeping from the pipes, which is going to be the important factor, the real essence of that work, is the carry over to other fields. That's where the strength of that work will be.

This 'seepage' is also reflected in the way Laura developed her National Curriculum 'world' topic. As indicated in earlier chapters, a class of 6- to 7-year-olds investigated worlds, learnt about our solar system, constructed their own worlds, discussed them and wrote about them. They investigated the effects of climate, growth and pollution on both the Earth and their worlds, and they prepared and performed a dance drama about the beginning of the world. This involved creating their own characters, designing and making their own costumes and learning a poem. Laura engaged in chemistry, as she put it, by attempting to dye some tights to reflect the characters the children had created for the dance drama:

There's a discussion about chemistry here. With the costumes they were very much being something, and their ideas are changing now so what we're going to do is, and this is, I suppose quite symbolic, we're going to strip out the colour in the tights and put in the things that we decide to put in. This will be to do with how the children feel about the movements they're making and what they're representing in the dance. So if they're thinking about the moon and we're going to have moon tights delight or it could be earthy, or it could be fire, wind, rain. It could be whatever they want to represent.

Laura, along with many other primary teachers, argued that children understand in holistic ways, and incorporating other experiences such as dance not only makes emotional connections with public knowledge but allows children to take more control over the process of engaging with knowledge:

I just think it's an activation. It's to do with respecting what they've got and allowing them to give shape to their feelings about things and their ideas and their desires about things and to let them grow and to let them come to fruition. Quite often, for young children the frustration of being a young child is not having the skills to develop things, particularly in art and creative work. They have wonderful visions as children, beautiful visions. The colour and shape and space, but they don't have the skills to produce what they have provisions for and I like us to be able to give them the skills but without losing the vision.

In Marilyn's Tudor topic, the Year 6 pupils learnt a musical, choreographed some dances, composed some Tudor music, visited Hampton

Court, watched part of the film of Columbus and a TV series, read 'fact finders', looked at some Shakespeare plays, learnt poems, wrote life stories, painted figures and made large collages of Elizabethan figures, constructed pirates, maps, props for the play, time lines, sand timers, compasses, listened to stories and put together an extensive topic folder. As Marilyn said, 'We've been rushing around everywhere. It's been fun but it's also interesting.' Laura's aims are used in topics which are defined in terms of themes rather than subject-centred topics.

A thematic approach

Wendy devised an architectural project which compared urban examples around the school with examples from a rural setting during a school journey. Her topic in the autumn term of 1992 was entitled Town and Country. She investigated this through the concept of environmental architecture. Her cross-curricular theme was broken into three parts – investigation of London urban architecture, work with a professional sculptor on designing school playground sculptures and comparative work in an urban setting on a school journey to Kent.

She enlisted the assistance of the Camden Arts Centre who had an exhibition of urban sculpture which focused on St Pancras Station. The children were taken to the station and workers from the Centre worked with the children on investigating the architecture from an aesthetic and functional perspective. Drawings and descriptions were encouraged; back in school these were integrated into the literacy curriculum and historical and geographical aspects were considered in the classroom activities. The Centre then provided the support of a professional sculptor, Mark, one morning a week for eight weeks, who worked with the children in designing some sculptures for the school environment. These models were either totally their own ideas, stimulated by focusing on the school exterior or evolved from working with the materials available. The children, after some discussion with the sculptor about how sculptures might enhance the school, toured the school environs looking for ideas of where to locate structures and consequently, how to construct their model and what materials to use. This did not, for some of the children, result in decisions immediately. Some structures evolved in the process of playing around with the materials provided, such as cylinders, card, fixatives including tape and string, and frames. Others evolved as they conversed in small groups or by observing other more defined plans, or as a result of chats with Mark. This process seemed to allow natural time for children to take control and ownership of their constructions rather than jumping to a timetable established by the teachers.

The pupils' constructions were stimulated by various reasons. Personal connections resulted in a world based on a theme of Australia because Carla had been there. James made a fishing rod because he fished in the local canal. Instrumental reasons assisted Eda in constructing a windmill to provide some electricity for a school sign, Sam to make an insect because he wanted to put something in the garden and Dwayne and John to make geometrical shapes for the nursery building. Constructions were also created during the process of using the materials. Abdul was putting Sellotape on some Plasticine and saw a magic wand emerging, Sirak spotted a stick that looked like a hockey stick and so he made a hockey player. Sean made a Red Indian because he found an old bow in the playground. A conceptual construction emerged from Kate's thinking:

We're going to Cardfields [school journey centre] so I thought we would phone home and our topic is town and country. So I thought I'd do two phones, one town and one country. I had an old phone at home. We were going to make a pencil and some rubbers but it wasn't very interesting so I said I've got a phone at home. How could we use that? I had to go around and find a modern phone. I asked my dad and my mum went to BT and they gave us an old one.

In this project, Wendy kept control of the process and extended the children's depth of experience of a specific subject, that is, sculpture.

The topic had a holistic dimension in that children's skills, experiences, interests, and 'reflections in action' were all part of the activity, and they shared discussion around differing approaches. This might be described as a more natural situation, one not dominated by the limitations of a single-subject investigation, involving a learning process which came more naturally to the children. The merging of this holistic curriculum approach with the National Curriculum has caused these particular teachers some considerable problems as Wendy indicates:

They're trying to match their sort of unworkable model with what actually goes on, which is basically project-based, theme-based teaching. Now to do that, what you have to do is a complete mind bend, put your brain cells in complete contortions to try and work out what you're actually doing, and what the spies know you're doing . . . they're imposing a secondary base model on primary schools. I wouldn't want to teach like that but it seems that is the logical conclusion of the National Curriculum. It undermines the teaching of the whole child until the age of 11. It splits them up into specialist subject based learning, not child-centred education. That is the only way I think you can actually teach the National Curriculum at junior level. That is not the way I want to teach at top junior level. But given the National Curriculum, that's the only way you could actually, practically, do it. It's not practical for class teachers to teach it that way. But then I probably wouldn't want to teach.

Embodying the basics

The teachers prioritize literacy and numeracy, and at the same time are keen to ensure that they do not unbalance the curriculum; as Alexander (1992) suggests the National Curriculum does in the excessive amount of time allotted for the core 'basics'. Wendy thought:

> within that, one's doing one's basics, a lot of language work, literacy, and I just think we should be specialists in teaching literacy and numeracy. Just as in secondary schools you have a history specialist. The National Curriculum's ignoring the fact that primary teachers are specialists in literacy and numeracy and that on top of that, a real interest in project learning to include history, geography, science, technology. As soon as you try to teach the specialisms of a secondary school, what's going to happen? – You're not going to have any literacy and numeracy taught because it's not like a 45-minute or a half-hour secondary English lesson . . . In the primary school you're teaching children how to read and write. It can be an all-day process. There's a lot of work to be done with them, and it's not just something you do in between doing other stuff.

Wendy ensured a literacy element to her projects. For example, the evacuation topic was predominantly a literacy topic involving book making, as indicated in Chapter 6. The construction of the story involved paired evaluations and the use of child editors as well as conferences with the teacher. Laura ensured that all the 'children's worlds' experiential work was written up; she worked with individuals and groups developing their writing. Grace organized her spellings around the St Lucia topic. Marilyn used relevant film and stories to investigate historical periods and the children had to evaluate them as film and literature reviews.

Thus these teachers sought to achieve coherence across the curriculum by incorporating other subjects into a topic from a particular subject area or by using cross-curricular themes. The latter may be harder to sustain within a subject-based National Curriculum, and the former may well become the predominant mode of working in primary schools in the future. However, this approach has its problems, according to Wendy, who specialized in science at college:

> I think it's too prescriptive to say they have done this bit of [electricity], that bit of magnetism at this stage, and I don't think that makes [sense]. Again, I think it's [a] completely reductionist attitude that if you teach science, the younger they are, the better scientist you're going to have. I don't think that is how people get inspired or develop in a career. I don't think teaching science early is going to give the country more scientists. I think having children who are engaged in their work and imaginative and enquiring minds is going to give you more scientists.

This argument is redolent of Popkewitz's (1994) description of the school curriculum as an 'alchemy' of phenomena. He is referring to how the individual disciplines are converted into school subjects bearing little resemblance to the features of creativity and imagination to which Wendy refers. In other words the curriculum becomes made up of 'imaginary subjects'.

A further problem is how the changing face of topic work entails a shift away from an entitlement curriculum (Webb 1993), and away from values, purposes and worthwhileness (Dadds 1994) towards simply delivery of a curriculum. In Dadds' view, less time means less time for divergent thinking and children who don't 'receive' the delivery the first time becoming problems rather than challenges. Wendy described how she saw her role:

> I feel most things that we do children can get a lot out of and most of them do. But there's always individuals in certain subjects who don't and for me this is a challenge. I had a child who was very bright in my class. For a whole term she wouldn't write anything although she was a brilliant reader. She really has a writer's block. I talked to her mother and we decided to have a head-on clash with her. It was a big emotional clash for the child but now she's got through that and now she writes reams. We found a way through. She said she didn't want to do it, she hated doing it. However, I wasn't going to say 'You don't have to do it because you don't like it.' It's the sensitivity to recognize it's an emotional problem as well for her in that situation.

Wendy here indicates how she saw this child as a challenge, and was determined not to let her become a problem. These teachers were neither soft in allowing pupils undue latitude, nor were they dogmatic about their attitude to a holistic curriculum. They recognized the differing subject epistemologies concerning, for example, the use of 'truth' in science (Dadds 1994). In the following examples, Laura uses scientific truth to affect children's decisions over food, and Grace explains how truth was tackled in their history project:

> We used to get, sort of magimix, a school dinner and a pudding and see what happens after the stomach had done it's bit, just to see what things look like. And we started checking on how much protein there was in their favourite things. Just those sorts of fairly simple categories, and so they found out, a little bit crude in a sense, how much muscle food they took in, how much energy food they took in. It was very important to them actually at the end of the day. And they started telling their parents what they were going to eat and refusing junk food . . . And it's actually informed quite a lot of the parents because we went and got all those brochures that you get from Sainsbury's and things about food, and also we did quite a lot of ecology things.

I thought it was actually making them think, things like whether Henry VIII was a good man – is that a fact, or is that an opinion?

Neither did these teachers deny the advantage that can be gained by pupils investigating phenomena in subject depth. In fact, they were very concerned that the breadth of the National Curriculum was causing a superficial covering of the curriculum. We enlarge upon this later.

KNOWLEDGE AS PROCESS

The National Curriculum focuses on ends to be attained, bodies of information, codified facts, theories and generalizations, measured products. This recalls the 'objectives model' of curriculum planning which dominated the 1950s and 1960s – the pre-Plowden era. Teaching was seen as a rational activity, subject to general principles and laws, that are discoverable through research. As we come to know them, so teaching can become more systematic, structured and stable. Our aims are inevitably value-orientated, but, as J.S. Mill observed, we have to 'hand [our ends] over to science' for the best methods of achieving them. The clearer we can specify our aims, the better. In one form, such thinking promotes the rational planning of a curriculum by objectives, which are harder-edged and more precise than general aims, and which, preferably, can be measured. This 'behavioural-objectives' model is the most prominent example of this approach, defining education as the 'changing of behaviour' (which includes thinking and feeling). As Sockett (1976: 17) points out, 'By eliminating the value aspect from the definition, the processes of education can be tackled by science. Furthermore, by making objectives measurable, you can see exactly what has been achieved, and what more needs to be done.'

Some have felt that these techniques are more appropriate for 'training' than for 'education', that they exert a constraining strait-jacket on teachers, and ignore the educational worth of processes as opposed to ends (Stenhouse 1975). They are more about efficiency than educational quality. Nor can they so easily be separated from values. Specifying objectives is useful for teacher accountability as well as assessing student achievement. The whole framework seems ready-made for the marketing ideology that has informed government policy in the 1980s and 1990s (Ball 1993). In short, the objectives model may represent a scientific means, but in respect of a highly specific and limited view of education.

Elliott (1991), following Stenhouse (1975), has spelled out the vastly different ideas on which the process model is based:

Questions about ends cannot be separated from questions about means; the value of human activities lies in their intrinsic qualities . . .

Activities are justified by their intrinsic ends, and these do not refer to observable effects . . . Rational action proceeds from practical deliberation about how to realize ends-in-view in concrete activities within particular complex situations . . .

(Elliott 1991: 137)

Clearly, it is to this model that our teachers heartily subscribe, in their insistence on helping pupils 'develop their intellectual powers by utilizing public structures of knowledge in constructing personal understandings of life situations'; focusing on the 'active construction rather than the passive reproduction of meaning'; facilitating 'the development of pupils' natural powers of understanding, rather than to produce certain predetermined performance outcomes' (pp. 150–1). How, then, did they manage the objectives modelled National Curriculum?

Process

Most of our teachers would claim that process continues to be the focus of their teaching. As Theresa said:

> If I say to parents, 'This piece of maths work is wrong, but I find it very encouraging because she [the pupil] will notice that the process was exactly right, and you see by the work this is very encouraging', you can see total disbelief on their faces.

Winsome, a science specialist, thought the National Curriculum science was too narrow and should be expanded 'fivefold'. She felt the expectations were too low because 'you have to kind of hop, skip and jump across too many attainment targets'. She would rather have an expanded science curriculum in which the teachers chose different topics but did them in depth. She argued that although the National Curriculum was often justified in terms of ensuring teachers didn't do the same thing with children time and time again, the reality was that children were doing electricity far more often in the new spiral curriculum. In her view:

> the point is not the knowledge, but the technique. The in-depth exploration, the scientific method, that's what you are after in young children. It doesn't actually matter whether you do it through looking at tadpoles, or making electrical circuits really, you are developing that enquiring mind, that enquiring spirit. And the most important point of any scientific work is to give children time for reflection and that is just what they don't get when you are expected to cover $x + 1$ numbers of attainment targets . . . Doing a few things in detail and depth and then you have something of quality rather than a superficial covering.

The connection with ends, and the priority of means is clear in Marilyn's mind:

I used to worry about people saying 'Oh God, they're doing Tudors and Stuarts again', but this idea of these bodies of knowledge that the National Curriculum is saying you do is at this age difficult for the children to put into context. They can't put them into chronological order really. The questions they ask make it perfectly obvious that they haven't got that ability yet. I think what I should be doing in terms of that is giving them the processes they need to go through to learn about those things.

The teachers do have a concept of process as knowledge, rather than just practical application of the curriculum. Laura, for example, was sure that learning could incorporate alternative perspectives:

Oh yes, absolutely, because learning is a dynamic. It isn't just taking something on board. If one could imagine a society which was never affected by any other society and was totally clear-cut about what it believed, was a purist society and you had the story of the creation, which was never questioned and children went in and took it on board, I don't think that they would develop very far. I think it's the whole idea that there are questions and that there's a dynamic of experience of stories. The power of stories is amazing. It's not just the stories we have in books. Exposing children to all of these, making them question is what creates all the thinking processes, all those cogs tumbling over like mad and eventually they'll mesh up.

This emphasis on process could not have been sustained without some strategic action. What, then, did this consist of?

Appropriation

This involves taking active control of the changes and responding to them in a creative, but selective way (Pollard *et al.* 1994; Woods 1995). Teachers select the process aspects of each subject and focus on them. Thus Grace developed an understanding of stereotyping and Winsome developed an interest in 'fair tests':

There was a week's worth of study in that, because once you've done the first tests and found a good shape for a boat, you realized you could vary materials, you could add sails and test all the various sails, add a keel, test the type of weight it loads. And although you're still in one area you're actually exploring a lot of scientific ideas and the scientific process. The temptation is, 'Oh gosh! We'd better move on and do a bit more.' Something different. Actually, I'm not going to. I'm going to stick with that idea we are covering in my classroom workshops, but I can see how the temptation would be to think, 'Well, we've had two weeks on boats, we'd better do something else'.

Developing empathy

Empathy is a prominent feature of these teachers' work. Marilyn uses atmosphere, issues, stories and arts subjects to express experiences:

> Being able to empathize is a huge part of their learning. I suppose it's because I'm a socially minded sort of person that I would want them to be able to look at people from all different spectrums, and have some sort of way of empathizing with them. And I'm not talking just about the arts. I think it's true of all areas of the curriculum that there is this behaviour which almost ensures that you have to be a learner. You will act like a mathematician, you will explore and investigate. That's in an area I'm finding hard to get them going on with our maths scheme with regard to the open-ended aspect of the investigation. They come up and say 'I've finished, I've done enough now' and I say. 'Oh, you can go on, you can go on and on and on and take this a bit further.' So this learning behaviour is being a scientist, being an artist.

After their performance, Nicola, a Year 6 pupil, talked about being two people:

> When we were on our way down to the hall I felt like I was a Tudor person. The way we had to walk made me feel like I was a Tudor person, but coming out of the hall afterwards although I knew I had done it, I still felt like a Tudor person. Everyone was looking at me and when we got in the back into the classroom I took all my clothes off and left the ones I had on underneath and it felt like I wasn't a Tudor any more. It just felt like I was me.

Asked what was good about playing somebody else, they replied:

Hayley: When I'm a Tudor person I miss being me and when I was me I missed being a Tudor.

Georgina: To see what they've done, experience how they live.

Karen: Yes, I reckon it is a good way how to learn history.

Katie: I would prefer to be myself but I would have liked to be like the real Henry VIII when he was living, to see what it was really like and not just playing the part.

Kim: When I was coming in and out of my costume, it felt like I was coming in and out of that time.

John, a boy who was very critical of his own achievements and often got upset at his own inadequacies, enjoyed the history musical a lot and indicated what other aspects of history interested him:

> I'd like to learn about cavemen times . . . How they got their food and how they made their weapons. How did the world begin. How

did people think because no one knows the truth about how people thought, no one knows. The thing about Adam and Eve could just be a big fairy tale . . . We don't hardly know anything about the past apart from family matters, because stories might have gone through the family telling a story.

He had clearly reflected on the nature of history. Other pupils confirmed this in conversation. They were convinced we knew very little of the past, though by introducing them to ways of recording evidence, for example film of the raising of the *Mary Rose*, they were beginning to build up a repertoire of methods for inquiry. The children became steeped in the subject and in one discussion with the researcher, one group began to explore their reactions to the topic. They first of all realized that there were differing perspectives of history, for many had been given one picture of Henry VIII's court by visits to the London Dungeon, and then they had been given another by visiting Hampton Court. Georgina commented: 'when we went to Hampton Court we found the other side of the story, really. We believed in one thing and it was not true.' They then explored how they could possibly find out the real truth by using information firstly from books. This was soon dismissed as unreliable by Kim: 'Yes, but how do the books know, how do they find out?' They next considered a TV programme concerned with the gathering of historical evidence from the Tudor ship, the *Mary Rose*, but even this was only seen as partial evidence: 'By bones they don't know, they only find out if he's fat and stuff like that.' Karen surmised that if the Tudors could only be partially known they might have been like them: 'The Tudors might have been like us. They could have gone to rave parties as well, they could have dressed like us.' Nicola then observed other similarities in terms of world-wide poverty: 'If you go out into other countries, they've got places where they keep children like slaves and they wear rags and clothes like some of the Tudor poor people who couldn't afford much.' They had a number of questions they wanted to explore, such as 'why they wanted to live like that', 'why they liked to execute, seems sick to me', 'why Henry VIII executed his wives'. They talked through the supposed affair Catherine Howard had with Sir Francis and Katie summed up their view:

Catherine was talking to Francis and one of the people, I don't know who it was, said that she, Catherine, was having an affair with Francis and so he's gone and told Henry VIII and he's executed Catherine because Henry didn't know both sides of the story.

This discussion goes on for some time and it ends with Georgina's view that she would 'prefer not to know a load of lies like different stories, I'd like to know the real thing, the thing that happened.'

Teachers provided new perspectives to be used, investigated and considered. At the same time, they wanted to ensure that the children took ownership of the new information and developed their interests and under-standings. However, the teachers were also keen to generate understandings about knowledge and how knowledge was socially constructed, as Laura observes:

> I worry that children are always looking for the right answer. They've got a feeling that somewhere there's the right answer and if only we knew it, everything will be all right. They imagine that I'm holding out on them, making them guess. What I want them to realize is that there's any right answer for them, and they have to decide on what it is. I don't expect them to be very conscious of this at the present time but I just feel that if the little seed is planted it's there, and it'll maybe get nurtured one day. That they have a right to make decisions for themselves and they have a right to their own opinion, and they have a right to decide what they think about things.

Winsome, a science-trained teacher, explained what she would like to do:

> I feel it should be 'Do they know this law? Have they got this un-derstanding?' rather than 'Have they got this fact?' The emphasis is still very much on that. If we want to help young children to develop their scientific thinking, particularly at key stage 1, we should really be giving them an opportunity to follow their own ideas and refine them and work on something in depth. But I think at the moment the present National Curriculum is neither one thing nor the other. It's still very heavily prescribed. In the end, pressurized teachers are going to say 'I must make sure I cover these statements' and their programmes of study are just a guide to the kind of style and topic. So, if you were going to, say, look at 'life processes', I think it would be more important to say that children at key stage 1 should develop an understanding of the primates, the life and interconnection be-tween living things on this planet and maybe life sources – I'm just plucking at ideas in mid-air. So that could be the aim of that attain-ment target. And then as far as specifying what's studied . . . it would be better to say, within this umbrella . . . children should study the 'living earth' or the 'processes of life'.

BREADTH AND BALANCE

The National Curriculum promised breadth and balance to which all chil-dren were entitled – an idea that had widespread support. Here was a statutory curriculum in which all foundation subjects, not just the basics, were allocated time. Delivery of this dream turned out, however, to be a nightmare, mainly, in the first instance, because of it being unbalanced in terms of overload (Campbell 1993a). As Galton (1995: 40) observes, 'the decision to allow each subject panel to design a "broad and balanced curriculum", without the availability of any responsible body to oversee its collective impact on the primary school, resulted in a crisis situation'. There were other problems. Teachers were asked to reconcile two distinct values, that of a broad curriculum as a right for all children on the one hand, with the wish to develop skills, interests and knowledge in depth on the other. Kelly and Blenkin (1993) point to the intellectual incoherence of prescribing a curriculum which will minister to every child's particular needs. Yet another contradiction has been noted by Campbell (1993a), who argues that the emphasis on testing and the publication of results led to even more of a concentration on the 'basics' at the expense of other subjects, though this particular point is not true of our teachers.

It also caused other problems. The emphasis was on individual assessment, and consequently proof needed to be produced by teachers of pupils having covered specific topics and having understood the knowledge involved. This can, in teachers' views, only be achieved by the compilation of copious records and providing written evidence from the children that they have engaged with the topic, usually in the form of worksheets or written descriptions. Laura noted:

> teachers are being structured by the paperwork, and if you're moving to a system in which we keep records, *x* number of attainment targets with so many different levels, that is how you structure your work – so that you can keep those records. In a sense it's being imposed in that way, because if you work my way it's not possible to keep records without some gargantuan task every evening.

This bureaucratic aspect individualizes the curriculum in terms of ability rather than encouraging common experiences through speculation and evaluation. Campbell's (1993b: 225) view that 'the broad and balanced curriculum cannot be delivered' seems not unreasonable.

There are a number of problems, therefore, for teachers aiming to provide coverage of the curriculum, but who also feel that the individual child's particular needs and depth of treatment are also important concerns. The following strategies were noted among our teachers.

Staggered entry

In this approach children begin investigations or projects at different times. Laura's 6- to 7-year-olds began the construction of their own worlds over three to four weeks. These worlds were part of her topic on the solar system. During the summer term the class prepared a dance drama concerning the birth of a world and they began to construct their own worlds out of junk and rubbish. The children had been asked to bring in any used containers and boxes from home. On an A3 flat piece of card the children were encouraged to construct fantasy worlds in 3D. Various experiments were tried to manipulate the material, and strategies were shared on how to attach models to the card. As time went on, it was suggested by one of the children that these worlds might be enclosed in boxes. This took off, and a wide range of literally open and closed worlds were created. The children discussed their models regularly and they were asked to write about them. Characters were introduced through teaching them how to make figures with newspaper and tape.

First starters were able to refine their original ideas in the light of later discussions. It also suited some children who were a little unsure about starting directions to watch and see how other children worked. It also allowed some depth to develop in that later starters built on the development of ideas over time. Ideas were constantly being taken up by later starters and refined. This led to restarts by children whereby they were encouraged to talk all the time about their worlds. If they felt they wanted to change them, they were allowed to do so providing they explained their reasons.

Marilyn talks about the advantages of a staggered entry approach for her:

> Yes, it's interesting, isn't it, because they're not all going to enter it at the same point because they'll see what other groups are doing and there'll be a development, it's sort of a rolling entry as well. Each group can advance that bit faster really . . . The other advantage is time and energy for me. Also there are certain things that you can't really contemplate doing as a class. Then, I think there's the quality of discussion for those children who don't take part in a large group. Certainly you can draw in children that might not contribute to the class discussion usually, because you've remembered something that's happened in their group . . . they get more depth, and they keep coming back, sort of revisiting I think.

Laura also talks about the value of children using each others' ideas:

> You see this is a problem, the notion of copying. We've got to get over this idea, this negative thing about copying. I have to get over this, 'Oh they're just copying each other if they're working together'. This isn't what it is, it's learning. If two children are working together and one has got brilliant ideas and the other one has a go at using their brilliant ideas and taking them on board as their own, that's a sort of common knowledge isn't it? . . . The next time this child is in the situation where it needs a few ideas, it's got a springboard, it's learnt a construct, it's learnt what ideas are. It's got a springboard to go from and it could maybe work with another child and be the producer of ideas. You don't have to have the same children working together all the time, it's not the same person who's leader each time

if you swap them around. I think the idea of children writing with
their arm round their work is really, really silly and it took me a long
time to get over the feeling that copying is a negative thing.

This is a good illustration of constructivist learning theory (Vygotsky
1978) in practice. The staggered entry organization ensures that collaboration between pupils takes place. Firstly, it may be associative – discussing
ideas generally as well as in particular relation to their own specific project (Dowrick 1993). Also alliances are formed to construct joint worlds,
although it doesn't matter if they then split to go it alone, as Natalie (Year
2) indicates: 'I took off the magic towers and Ashley used my fountain. I
said she could because I didn't want it and that was in this place that I'm
painting now.'
   Collaboration, secondly, doesn't have to be a joint problem-solving activity with only one defined outcome. It can be exploratory with different pupils using trial-and-error strategies together on their own materials.
This sort of approach may be more successful in terms of collaboration
because the children have more control over an activity from the beginning.
   Thirdly, children's contributions are valued and help to develop the
project. Some of the pupils in Laura's class were discussing how Rosa
could show both sun and snow on her world and it was suggested by
Kayla that a box might enclose the world and then it could be done.
Ever conscious of integrating her curriculum, Laura altered her maths
programme to include some mathematics on boxes. Collaboration was
also a central theme of the dance drama group constructions in that groups
of children had to create joint dances.
   This form of organization makes the time available more elastic, because for most of the day there is always someone working on a model,
and other children are able to absorb the discussions and developments
as they engage with other tasks, using those experiences later when it
comes to the revisiting of their model. It is this feature of creating time
that ensures reflection and evaluation. The time that is created by Laura
is not just opportunities for revisiting, renewal, reflection and developing
ownership. Space is created for developing language. Vocabulary grows
as children are expected constantly to explain their creations to her or to
small and large groups. Here the children articulate descriptions and in
doing so Laura is able to assist by introducing technical terms such as
'netting', 'folding', 'spirals'.
   These descriptions are created in the 'pedagogic moment' by the child
in reaction to the teachers' question. Whilst the child may have some idea
of what is happening in her model or what kind of character her dancer
is going to be, we have observed that more often than not they create
these characters in response to the open questions the teacher asks them.
So it is a creative process, not only an information extraction process. Also

the teacher brings in other relevant variables: how will you attach it, is it suitable for dancing, where does the water go from here? This encourages discussion and debate, particularly in group sessions, as the next example shows.

Here, Laura is talking to Natalie about her world with a group watching. At the end she asks if anyone else has got any questions for Natalie:

Laura: And a pond there, are there any creatures living in your pond? Can you tell me what sort of creatures?

Natalie: Fish, crabs and jellyfish.

Laura: Really, any other sorts of creatures?

Natalie: And a mermaid.

Laura: A mermaid. And what about in the sea?

Natalie: The sea is full of different coloured fish and mermaids. And there's a little river coming under there which . . .

Laura: An underground river, eh?

Natalie: It comes under there and up to the pond. The mermaids go under there, they go under this little rock and they just wish.

Laura: They wish.

Natalie: Yes.

Laura: What sort of wishes?

Natalie: Any wish they want.

Laura: Well, tell me one that they've made.

Natalie: Well, the mermaid made one that she wanted a white bird and it came true.

Laura: Oh, the mermaid wished for a white bird and it came true, is that your white bird there?

Natalie: Yes.

Laura: And the bird came because of a wish by the mermaid. OK, has anybody got any questions they want to ask Natalie about this?

Absher: Why don't the fish have a wish?

Natalie: They do.

Laura: Oh, they do. What sort of things do the fish wish for?

Natalie: They wish for seaweed and homes under the water.

Laura: What sort of homes under the water?

Natalie: Shells.

Laura: Shells, that's interesting. What sort of fish live in shells under the water?

Natalie: But mermaids live in these great big shells and they're really deep under the water.

Natalie is unaware of the questions that are going to be asked, yet she replies with the utmost confidence, constructing the scene as the interchange progresses. This elasticity of time is only possible in a class teaching situation where a variety of subjects are pursued. In a more specialist, once-a-week session, the activities have a limited time period for engagement and reflection.

Revisiting

These teachers have a number of investigations or activities going on over a considerable period of time. The pupils look forward to reclaiming their work and, in some cases, they are encouraged to change direction, as in the 'Worlds' topic in Laura's class, if they think it is appropriate. Some drawings of artefacts in Tudor times were amended or reworked by Year 6 pupils in Marilyn's class over many weeks. This approach allowed reflection, and chances to discuss new methods or ideas with others. Jamie liked the amount of time he had to spend on his picture of a Tudor person, which enabled him 'to be nice and careful and to put in lots of detail. Taking a long time means I try and do my best and therefore I need to work slowly.' Simon (Year 2) told us 'that finishing off my work I didn't complete the day before' was what he looked forward to when coming to school in the morning. Ashley (Year 2) was asked how others knew she had worked hard and she, like others, talked about time being an important factor in the quality of her outcomes 'because you weren't rushing it. Because Laura would know because we usually do it neatly.'

Eddie is adamant that revisiting projects has enormous benefits:

> I remember taking them on a school journey to Sayers Croft, and we spent an afternoon just sketching various buildings in the village and bringing these sketches back to school with photographic evidence. From those pen and ink drawings and photographs three children actually made 3D houses that were so big, initially, they didn't have a clue as to how to go about it. The experimentation was really messy, you know, making the walls so that they would all fit together, making the type of brickwork that a particular house had . . . Walls were collapsing and we were stuffing the house with paper because they understood that the paper would burn off in the kiln. The roof would sag in and so in turn they had to measure it and there was a hell of a lot of work involved and luckily when they were actually fired they actually worked. And then we were able to plan a roadway and make the gardens with the fencing. Visually it was brilliant and for the children themselves it was like 'I have done this'. So although there was not much recording, the actual process was quite fulfilling and it involved a lot of thinking, a lot of planning, a lot of experimenting and the result was out of this world. But it took a long time. I think these children were at the stage where they didn't have to have immediate results. The sketches and the drawings were immediate

results and they were quite fulfilled about that, but they were quite capable of working on something long term, without wanting that immediate result.

The compression of time under intensification is talked of by A. Hargreaves (1994), in which instantaneous results are expected and where control over the learning process shifts from the learner to the bureaucracy of time constraints. Strategies such as 'staggered entry' and 'revisiting' get round this problem to some extent.

Workshop investigations

Workshops involve different groups or individuals investigating different aspects of a particular phenomenon or issue. Ian, a sixth-year pupil, wanted to merge the Tudor topic with his interest in maps and so he, unlike the others in his class, worked on a map of sea explorations at the same time. Nevertheless they all benefited from his efforts through discussions concerning the geography of the world in Tudor times and information concerning the routes taken by the Tudor explorers.

The investigation of the volume of the giant's bowl mentioned earlier was carried out by Kayla and a group of children from Laura's 6- to 7-year-old class. They were asked to discover the relationship between linear measurement and volume by measuring the capacity of a giant's bowl the children had made which was twice the size of a child's bowl. This activity was prefaced by a discussion with the whole class. Laura stopped the focus group – the children directly involved – from time to time, asking them to identify any problems they were encountering. The supportive group – the rest of the class – asked questions, offered ideas, and these were discussed by the whole class. At the end of the activity, a class evaluation was carried out on the outcomes of the investigation. In another example, Eddie asked his children to make different sorts of clocks using water, sand and the sun, and the same process as Laura's was used to review and evaluate each other's activities. This approach ensured some hands-on activities from the investigating groups, but the teacher expected some of the children to think through the ideas without direct experience of that particular activity. It is not necessary for every child to be involved directly in every detail of an investigation. Children can enter the 'world of ideas' (Popper and Eccles 1977) without necessarily playing a full part in an investigation.

Winsome was asked what her Year 2 children liked about the way she organized her topic. She thought

they like the fact that there might be more than one activity going on. I might set up, for example, making magnetic games. They'd explored magnets a lot and properties of magnets, tested lots of materials and tested magnets working through water, and then using that knowledge we divided into groups. We talked it through, and they had to make a game given that you know magnets can work under water. They ended up making magnetic boats and making magnetic games, like a magnetic fishing game, given that they know that a magnet can work through cardboard. They made fishing rods and little fish. So the children were able to choose which game they wanted to make. So in making magnetic toys, there was an element of choice, and I think they find it stimulating to watch what the others were doing. Then we had a session where they showed each other what they'd done.

In a Year 6 class, a group of children constructed a play concerning smoking on 'no smoking day', and the class discussed the issue later. Here again, the non-active pupils experienced the depth of this activity vicariously, though they did engage in the discussions. This may appear to be an individualized curriculum, but the skill of the teacher to manage that diversity is the key. In this approach a variety of experiences and perspectives were encouraged.

Depth and breadth in quantifiable terms could be achieved through the National Curriculum, though the road leads to specialism because of the quantity and prescriptive nature of the attainment targets in these teachers' eyes. An alternative approach is underpinned by an emphasis on the quality of learning which can also achieve breadth and depth. But it must rely on varied investigations in the classrooms, and the opportunity to discuss, evaluate and develop the investigations.

CONCLUSION

Teachers managed the curriculum with a mixture of pragmatism and principle. As long as there was room for sufficient of the latter to be there, they could meet the various problems thrown up by the old National Curriculum with skill and resolution. Marilyn and Laura articulate their values, which continue to find expression in their teaching:

I want them [the children] to feel they want to be there and I want them to enjoy what they're doing. I want them to know as well that they're responsible for their learning at the end of the day. That I can be there and I can tell them till I'm blue in the face or whatever, but at the end of the day they've got to do it. And I think everything I do, perhaps a lot of what I do then, revolves around that central thing that they have to be responsible for their learning. I can't do it for them.

I think it's right because I think it's right. Because at the end of the day, when you've had all the intellectual discussions with yourself, when you've compared all the values from different cultures and different societies, you look and you think 'This is the right way to behave'. At the end of the day you make a moral judgement about what you think is good . . . people being able to behave kindly to each other, with care and consideration for other people, and to develop their way of thinking. To develop themselves as persons seems to me to be a good thing. Because of that I think they might find a niche in almost any society.

The 1988 National Curriculum has now been slimmed down (Dearing 1994). 'Statements of attainment' have been replaced with 'level descriptions', signalling the abolition of the 'tick-box approach', a term that became common usage to describe the practice whereby teachers were reduced to ticking hundreds of little boxes under attainment target headings, rather than focusing on programmes of study.

This, then, is a distinct swing in the direction of process and away from objectives and technical rationality, to such an extent that Wragg (1995: 3), a persistent and outspoken critic of the changes, now feels that 'The new curriculum, with less detailed prescription and more emphasis on the programmes of study, allows schools to resurrect the HMI notion of "areas of experience" if they so wish.'

Coherence, holism and process could well come back into favour, it would seem, and be less matters of strategic adaptation for teachers. On the other hand, Galton (1995) argues that Dearing neglected certain key issues, namely, 'entitlement'; the issue of 'broad and balanced' against excellence or depth; the culture of primary schooling, particularly with reference to grouping practices, Galton arguing (p. 47) that primary teachers 'will continue to "graft" the programmes of study onto their existing pedagogy to create a hybridized version'; and the implications of the changes for the distribution of resources. The recommendation by Dearing that there should be no more change for five years is seen by Golby (1994: 102) as 'surely a triumph of hope over experience'. The National Curriculum has clearly moved into a second phase, more favourable to our teachers than the first, but we are still some way from a settled state – itself now rather a problematic concept. In these circumstances, teachers need to retain a sharp edge on their strategic repertoire.

REFERENCES

Abbs, P. (1989) Signs on the way to understanding, *Times Educational Supplement,* 10 November, p. 15.

Acker, S. (1994) *Gendered Education.* Buckingham: Open University Press.

Acker, S. (1995) Carry on caring: the work of women teachers, *British Journal of Sociology of Education,* 16 (1): 21–36.

Alexander, R.J. (1992) *Policy and Practice in Primary Education.* London: Routledge.

Alexander, R.J., Rose, J. and Woodhead, C. (1992) *Curriculum Organisation and Classroom Practice in Primary Schools: A Discussion Paper.* London: HMSO.

Apple, M.W. (1986) *Teachers and Texts: A Political Economy of Class and Gender Relations in Education.* New York: Routledge and Kegan Paul.

Apple, M.W. (1993) *Official Knowledge: Democratic Education in a Conservative Age.* London: Routledge.

Aspland, R. and Brown, G. (1993) Keeping teaching professional, in D. Bridges and T. Kerry (eds) *Developing Teachers Professionally.* London: Routledge.

Atkinson, P. and Delamont, S. (1977) Mock-ups and cock-ups: the stage-management of guided discovery instruction, in P. Woods and M. Hammersley (eds) *School Experience.* London: Croom Helm.

Baker, C. and Perrott, C. (1988) The news session in infants and primary school classrooms, *British Journal of Sociology of Education,* 9 (1): 19–38.

Ball, S.J. (1990) *Politics and Policy Making in Education.* London: Routledge.

Ball, S.J. (1993) Education markets, choice and social class: the market as a class strategy in the UK and the USA, *British Journal of Sociology of Education,* 14 (1): 3–19.

Ball, S.J. (1994) *Education Reform: A Critical and Post-structural Approach.* Buckingham: Open University Press.

Ball, S.J. and Bowe, R. (1992) Subject departments and the 'implementation' of National Curriculum policy: an overview of the issues, *Journal of Curriculum Studies,* 24 (2): 97–115.

Bennett, N. (1976) *Teaching Styles and Pupil Progress.* London: Open Books.

Berger, P.L. and Luckmann, T. (1967) *The Social Construction of Reality: A Treatise in the Sociology of Knowledge.* Harmondsworth: Penguin.

Berlak, A. and Berlak, H. (1981) *The Dilemmas of Schooling.* London: Methuen.

Bernstein, B. (1971) On the classification and framing of educational knowledge, in M.F.D. Young (ed.) *Knowledge and Control.* London: Collier Macmillan.

Bernstein, B. (1975) *Class, Codes and Control, Vol. 3: Towards a Theory of Educational Transmissions.* London: Routledge and Kegan Paul.

Bolton, E. (1993) Perspectives on the National Curriculum, in P. O'Hear and J. White (eds) *Assessing the National Curriculum.* London: Paul Chapman.

Bolton, G. (1994) Stories at work: fictional-critical writing as a means of professional development, *British Educational Research Journal,* 20 (1): 55–68.

Bonnett, M. (1991) Developing children's thinking . . . and the national curriculum, *Cambridge Journal of Education,* 21 (3): 277–92.

Bourne, J. (ed.) (1994) *Thinking Through Primary Practice.* London: Routledge.

Brehony, K. (1992) What's left of progressive primary education, in A. Rattansi and D. Reeder (eds) *Rethinking Radical Education: Essays in Honour of Brian Simon.* London: Lawrence and Wishart.

Bridges, D. (1994) 'Education and the market place: the nature of the argument', paper presented at the BERA Conference, Oxford, September.

Bruner, J. (1972) *Relevance of Education.* Harmondsworth: Penguin.

Bruner, J. (1986) *Actual Minds, Possible Worlds.* London: Harvard University Press.

Burgess, H. and Carter, B. (1992) Bringing out the best in people: teacher training and the 'real teacher', *British Journal of Sociology of Education,* 13 (2): 349–59.

Burwood, L.R.V. (1992) Can the national curriculum help reduce working class under-achievement?, *Educational Studies,* 18 (3): 311–21.

Campbell, R. (1992) *Reading Real Books.* Buckingham: Open University Press.

Campbell, R.J. (1993a) The National Curriculum in primary schools: a dream at conception, a nightmare at delivery, in C. Chitty and B. Simon *Education Answers Back: Critical Responses to Government Policy.* London: Lawrence and Wishart.

Campbell, R.J. (1993b) The broad and balanced curriculum in primary schools: some limitations on reform, *The Curriculum Journal,* 4 (2): 215–29.

Campbell, R.J. and Neill, S.R. St J. (1994) *Curriculum Reform at Key Stage 1 – Teacher Commitment and Policy Failure.* Harlow: Longman.

Campbell, R.J., Evans, L., Neill, S.R. St J. and Packwood, A. (1991a) *Workloads, Achievement and Stress: Two Follow-up Studies of Teacher Time in Key Stage 1.* Warwick: Policy Analysis Unit, Department of Education, University of Warwick.

Campbell, R.J., Evans, L., Neill, S.R. St J. and Packwood, A. (1991b) 'The use and management of infant teachers' time – some policy issues', paper presented at Policy Analysis Unit Seminar, Warwick, November.

Carr, W. (1989) *Quality in Teaching: Arguments for a Reflective Profession.* Lewes: Falmer.

Chitty, C. (1993) Managing a coherent curriculum: four case studies, in C. Chitty (ed.) *The National Curriculum: Is It Working?* London: Longman.

Clark, C.M. (1992) Teachers as designers in self-directed professional development, in A. Hargreaves and M.G. Fullan (eds) *Understanding Teacher Development.* London: Cassell.

Cockburn, A. (1994) Teachers' experience of time: some implications for future research, *British Journal of Educational Studies,* 42 (4): 375–87.

Coles, M. (1994) 'Critical enquiry and text talk in primary schools', paper presented at the BERA Conference, Oxford, September.

Collingwood, R.G. (1966) Expressing one's emotions, in E.W. Eisner and D.W. Ecker (eds) *Readings in Art Education*. Lexington, MA: Xerox College Publishing.

Corno, L. (1989) Self regulated learning, in B.J. Zimmerman and D.H. Schunk (eds) *Self Regulated Learning and Academic Achievement: Theory, Research and Practice*. New York: Springer-Verlag.

Dadds, M. (1994) The changing face of topic work in the primary curriculum, *The Curriculum Journal*, 4 (2): 253–66.

Dale, R. (1989) *The State and Education Policy*. Buckingham: Open University Press.

Davies, B. and Harré, R. (1990) Positioning: conversation and the production of selves, *Journal for the Theory of Social Behaviour*, 20 (1): 43–63.

Dearing, R. (1994) *Review of the National Curriculum: Final Report*. London: School Curriculum and Assessment Authority.

Delamont, S. (1976) *Interaction in the Classroom*. London: Methuen.

Deleuze, G. and Guattari, F. (1977) *Anti-Oedipus, Capitalism and Schizophrenia*. New York: Viking Press.

Department of Education and Science (1985) *The Curriculum from 5 to 16*. London: HMSO.

Dewey, J. (1929) *The Quest for Certainty: A Study of the Relation of Knowledge and Action*. New York: Minton, Balch.

Dowrick, N. (1993) Side by side: a more appropriate form of peer interaction for infant pupils?, *British Educational Research Journal*, 19 (5): 499–515.

Drummond, M.J. (1991) The child and the primary curriculum – from policy to practice, *The Curriculum Journal*, 2 (2): 115–24.

Edwards, A.D. and Furlong, V.J. (1978) *The Language of Teaching*. London: Heinemann.

Edwards, D. and Mercer, N. (1987) *Common Knowledge: The Development of Understanding in the Classroom*. London: Methuen.

Egan, K. (1988) *Teaching as Storytelling – An Alternative Approach to Teaching and the Curriculum*. London: Routledge.

Egan, K. (1992) *Imagination in Teaching and Learning: Ages 8–15*. London: Routledge.

Egan, K. and Nadaner, D. (eds) (1988) *Imagination and Education*. Milton Keynes: Open University Press.

Eisner, E.W. (1979) *The Educational Imagination*. London: Collier Macmillan.

Eisner, E.W. (1985) *The Art of Educational Evaluation: A Personal View*. Lewes: Falmer Press.

Eisner, E.W. (1993) Forms of understanding and the future of educational research, *Educational Researcher*, 22 (7): 5–11.

Elbaz, F. (1992) Hope, attentiveness, and caring for difference: the moral voice in teaching, *Teaching and Teacher Education*, 8 (5/6): 421–32.

Elliott, J. (1991) *Action Research for Educational Change*. Milton Keynes: Open University Press.

Epstein, D. (1993) Defining accountability in education, *British Educational Research Journal*, 19 (3): 243–59.

Fine, G.A. (1994) Working the hyphens: reinventing the self and other in qualitative research, in N. Denzin and Y. Lincoln (eds) *Handbook of Qualitative Research*. London: Sage.

Fitz, J. (1994) Implementation research and education policy: practice and prospects, *British Journal of Education Studies*, 42 (1): 53–69.

Flanders, N. (1970) *Analysing Teacher Behaviour.* New York: Addison-Wesley.

Foucault, M. (1970) *The Birth of the Clinic.* New York: Vintage.

Foucault, M. (1975) *Discipline and Punish.* Harmondsworth: Penguin.

Foucault, M. (1977) *The Archeology of Knowledge.* London: Tavistock.

Foucault, M. (1979) *A History of Sexuality.* Harmondsworth: Penguin.

Fox, C. (1989) Children thinking through story, *English in Education,* 23 (2): 33–42.

Fullan, M.G. (1992) *Successful School Improvement.* Buckingham: Open University Press.

Galton, M. (1995) Crisis in the Primary Classroom. London: David Fulton.

Galton, M. and Simon, B. (eds) (1980) *Progress and Performance in the Primary Classroom.* London: Routledge and Kegan Paul.

Gilmore, S. (1990) Art worlds: developing the interactionist approach to social organization, in H.S. Becker and M.M. McCall (eds) *Symbolic Interaction and Cultural Studies.* Chicago: University of Chicago Press.

Gipps, C. (1992) *What We Know About Effective Primary Teaching.* London: Institute of Education, Tufnell Press.

Giroux, H. (1992) *Border Crossings – Cultural Workers and the Politics of Education.* New York: Routledge.

Gitlin, A.D. (1990) Education research, voice and school change, *Harvard Educational Review,* 60 (4): 443–66.

Glaser, B.G. and Strauss, A.L. (1967) *The Discovery of Grounded Theory.* London: Weidenfeld and Nicolson.

Golby, M. (1994) After Dearing: a critical review of the Dearing Report, *The Curriculum Journal,* 4 (1): 95–105.

Graham, H. (1991) The concept of caring in feminist research: the case of domestic service, *Sociology,* 25 (1): 61–78.

Grumet, M. (1988) *Bitter Milk: Women and Teaching.* Amherst, MA: University of Massachusetts Press.

Halliwell, S. (1993) Teacher creativity and teacher education, in D. Bridges and T. Kerry (eds) *Developing Teachers Professionally: Reflections for Initial and In-service Trainers.* London: Routledge.

Hansen, D.T. (1993) The moral importance of the teacher's style, *Journal of Curriculum Studies,* 25 (5): 397–421.

Hargreaves, A. (1984) Contrastive Rhetoric and Extremist Talk, in A. Hargreaves and P. Woods (eds) *Classrooms and Staffrooms.* Milton Keynes: Open University Press.

Hargreaves, A. (1992) Curriculum reform and the teacher, *The Curriculum Journal,* 2 (3): 249–58.

Hargreaves, A. (1994) *Changing Teachers, Changing Times – Teacher's Work and Culture in the Postmodern Age.* London: Cassell.

Hargreaves, A. and Tucker, E. (1991) Teaching and guilt: exploring the feelings of teaching, *Teaching and Teacher Education,* 7 (5/6): 491–505.

Hargreaves, D.H. (1983) The teaching of art and the art of teaching: towards an alternative view of aesthetic learning, in M. Hammersley and A. Hargreaves (eds) *Curriculum Practice: Some Sociological Case Studies.* Lewes: Falmer Press.

Hargreaves, D.H. (1991) Coherence and manageability: reflections on the National Curriculum and cross-curricular provision, *The Curriculum Journal,* 2 (1): 33–41.

Hargreaves, D.H. (1994) The new professionalism: the synthesis of professional and institutional development, *Teaching and Teacher Education*, 10 (4): 423–38.

Harvey, D. (1989) *The Condition of Postmodernity*. Oxford: Blackwell.

Hatcher, R. (1994) Market relationships and the management of teachers, *British Journal of Sociology of Education*, 15 (1): 41–62.

Highet, G. (1951) *The Art of Teaching*. London: Methuen.

Howe, A. and Johnson, J. (eds) (1992) *Common Bonds: Storytelling in the Classroom*. (An account of the National Oracy Project.) London: Hodder and Stoughton.

Inglis, F. (1989) Managerialism and morality: the corporate and the republican school, in W. Carr (ed.) *Quality in Teaching: Arguments for a Reflective Profession*. London: Falmer.

Jackson, P.W. (1992) *Untaught Lessons*. New York: Teachers' College Press.

Johnson, J.J. (1990) *Selecting Ethnographic Informants*. London: Sage.

Keddie, N. (1971) Classroom knowledge, in M.F.D. Young (ed.) *Knowledge and Control*. London: Collier Macmillan.

Kelly, V. and Blenkin, G. (1993) Never mind the quality: feel the breadth and balance, in R. Campbell (ed.) *Breadth and Balance in the Primary Curriculum*. London: Falmer.

Kincheloe, J.L. (1993) *Towards a Critical Politics of Teacher Thinking*. London: Bergin and Garvey.

King, R.A. (1978) *All Things Bright and Beautiful*. Chichester: Wiley.

Kounin, J.S. (1970) *Discipline and Group Management in Classrooms*. New York: Holt, Rinehart and Winston.

Lacey, C. (1976) Problems of sociological fieldwork: a review of the methodology of 'Hightown Grammar', in M. Hammersley and P. Woods (eds) *The Process of Schooling*. London: Routledge and Kegan Paul.

Lasch, S. (1990) *Sociology of Postmodernism*. London: Routledge.

Lewin, K.R., Lippitt, R. and White, R.K. (1939) Patterns of aggressive behaviour in three 'social climates', *Journal of Social Psychology*, 10: 271–99.

Lieberman, A. and Miller, L. (1984) *Teachers: Their World and Their Work*. Alexandria, VA: Association for Supervision and Curriculum Development.

Lortie, D.C. (1975) *Schoolteacher*. Chicago: University of Chicago Press.

Lyotard, J.F. (1984) *The Postmodern Condition: A Report on Knowledge*. Manchester: Manchester University Press.

Mac an Ghaill, M. (1992) Teachers' work: curriculum restructuring, culture, power and comprehensive schooling, *British Journal of Sociology of Education*, 13 (2): 177–99.

McCall, M.M. and Wittner, J. (1990) 'The good news about life history', in H.S. Becker, and M.M. McCall (eds) *Symbolic Interaction and Cultural Studies*. Chicago: University of Chicago Press.

MacIntyre, A. (1981) *After Virtue*. London: Duckworth.

Mackey, S. (1993) Emotion and cognition in arts education, *Curriculum Studies*, 1 (2): 245–56.

McLean, M. (1992) *The Promise and Perils of Educational Comparison*. London: Institute of Education, Tufnell Press.

McNamara, D. (1990) The National Curriculum: an agenda for research, *British Educational Research Journal*, 16 (3): 225–35.

Maguire, M. and Ball, S. (1994) Discourses of educational reform in the United Kingdom and the USA and the work of teachers, *British Journal of Inservice Education*, 20 (1): 5–16.

Maw, J. (1993) The National Curriculum Council and the whole curriculum: reconstruction of a discourse?, *Curriculum Studies*, 1 (1): 55–74.

Mead, G.H. (1934) *Mind, Self and Society*. Chicago: University of Chicago Press.

Moffett, J. (1968) *Teaching the Universe of Discourse*. Boston: Houghton Mifflin Co.

Mortimore, P., Sammons, P., Lewis, L. and Ecob, R. (1988) *School Matters: The Junior Years*. London: Open Books.

National Curriculum Council (1989) *A Framework for the Primary Curriculum*. York: National Curriculum Council.

National Curriculum Council (1993) *The National Curriculum at Key Stages 1 and 2*. York: National Curriculum Council.

Nias, J. (1989) *Primary Teachers Talking*. London: Routledge.

Noddings, N. (1992) *The Challenge to Care in Schools: An Alternative Approach to Education*. New York: Teachers' College Press.

OFSTED (1993) *Curriculum Organisation and Classroom Practice in Primary Schools – A Follow Up Report*. London: DFE.

OFSTED (1994) *Science and Mathematics in Schools: A Review*. London: HMSO.

Olson, J. (1992) *Understanding Teaching: Beyond Expertise*. Buckingham: Open University Press.

Osborn, M. and Broadfoot, P. (1992) The impact of current changes in English primary schools on teacher professionalism, *Teachers' College Record*, 94 (1): 138–51.

Packwood, A. and Sikes, P. (1994) 'A postmodernist perspective on the personal realities of engaging in academic activities or every which way but loose', paper presented at the BERA Conference, Oxford, September.

Plowden Report (1967) *Children and their Primary Schools*, report of the Central Advisory Council for Education in England. London: HMSO.

Plummer, K. (1983) *Documents of Life*. London: Allen and Unwin.

Polanyi, M. and Prosch, H. (1975) *Personal Knowledge in Meaning*. London: University of Chicago Press.

Pollard, A. (1979) Negotiating deviance and 'getting done' in primary school classrooms, in L. Barton and R. Meighan (eds) *Schools, Pupils and Deviance*. Driffield: Nafferton Books.

Pollard, A. (1985) *The Social World of the Primary School*. London: Cassell.

Pollard, A. (1991) *Learning in Primary Schools*. London: Cassell.

Pollard, A., Broadfoot, P., Croll, P., Osborn, M. and Abbott, D. (1994) *Changing English Primary Schools? The Impact of the Education Reform Act at Key Stage One*. London: Cassell.

Popkewitz, T.S. (1994) Professionalisation in teaching and teacher education: some notes on its history, ideology and potential, *Teacher and Teacher Education*, 10 (1): 1–14.

Popper, K.R. and Eccles, J.C. (1977) *The Self and Its Brain*. Berlin: Springer International.

Poulson, L. (1994) 'The discourse of accountability: analysis of a key word in the process of implementing national curriculum policy in a core subject', paper presented at the BERA Conference, Oxford, September.

Reynolds, D. (1976) When teachers and pupils refuse a truce, in G. Mungham and G. Pearson (eds) *Working Class Youth Culture*. London: Routledge and Kegan Paul.

Richardson, L. (1994) Writing: a method of inquiry, in N.K. Denzin and Y.S. Lincoln (eds) *Handbook of Qualitative Research*. London: Sage.

Riseborough, G.F. (1981) Teacher careers and comprehensive schooling: an empirical study, *Sociology*, 15 (3): 352–81.

Riseborough, G.F. (1992) Primary headship, state policy and the challenge of the 1990s, *Journal of Education Policy*, 8 (2): 123–42.

Rogers, C. (1983) *Freedom to Learn for the 80s*. New York: Macmillan.

Ruddick, S. (1989) *Maternal Thinking: Towards a Politics of Peace*. New York: Ballantine.

Rutter, M., Maugham, B., Mortimore, P. and Ouston, J. (1979) *Fifteen Thousand Hours*. London: Open Books.

Schön, D.A. (1983) *The Reflective Practitioner: How Professionals Think in Action*. London: Temple Smith.

Schwab, J.J. (1969) The practical: a language for curriculum, *School Review*, 78: 1–24.

Sikes, P., Measor, L. and Woods, P. (1985) *Teacher Careers: Crises and Continuities*. Lewes: Falmer Press.

Simkins, T., Ellison, L. and Garrett, V. (eds) (1992) *Implementing Educational Reforms: The Early Lessons*. Harlow: Longman/BEMAS.

Simon, B. (1988) Why no pedagogy in England?, in R. Dale, R. Fergusson and A. Robinson (eds) *Frameworks for Teaching*. London: Hodder and Stoughton.

Siraj-Blatchford, I. (1993) Educational research and reform: some implications for the professional identity of early years teachers, *British Journal of Educational Studies*, 41 (4): 393–408.

Smyth, J. (1991) *Teachers as Collaborative Learners*. Buckingham: Open University Press.

Smyth, J. (1995) Teachers' work and the labor process of teaching: central problematics in professional development, in T.R. Guskey and M. Huberman (eds) *Professional Development in Education: New Paradigms and Practices*. New York: Teachers' College Press.

Sockett, H. (1976) Approaches to curriculum planning, Unit 16 of course E203, *Curriculum Design and Development*. Milton Keynes: Open University Press.

Steedman, C. (1988) The mother made conscious: the historical development of a primary school pedagogy, in M. Woodhead and A. McGrath *Family, School and Society*. London: Hodder and Stoughton.

Stenhouse, L. (1975) *An Introduction to Curriculum Research and Development*. London: Heinemann.

Strauss, A.L. and Corbin, J. (1990) *Basics of Qualitative Research: Grounded Theory Procedures and Techniques*. Newbury Park: Sage.

Thomas, C. (1993) De-constructing concepts of care, *Sociology*, 27: 649–69.

Tobias, S. (1994) Interest, prior knowledge and learning, *Review of Educational Research*, 64 (1): 37–54.

Tom, A. (1984) *Teaching as a Moral Craft*. New York: Longman.

Tom, A. (1988) Teaching as a moral craft, in R. Dale, R. Fergusson and A. Robinson (eds) *Frameworks for Teaching*. London: Hodder and Stoughton.

Tripp, D. (1993) *Critical Incidents in Teaching: Developing Professional Judgement*. London: Routledge.

Troman, G. (1996) No entry signs: educational change and some problems encountered in negotiating entry to educational settings, *British Educational Research Journal* (forthcoming).

Vulliamy, G. and Webb, R. (1993) Progressive education and the National Curriculum: findings from a global education research project, *Educational Review*, 45 (1): 21–41.

Vygotsky, L.S. (1978) *Mind in Society: The Development of Higher Psychological Processes*. London: Harvard University Press.

Walkerdine, V. (1986) Progressive pedagogy and political struggle, *Screen*, 27 (5): 54–60.

Walkerdine, V. (1989) Femininity as performance, *Oxford Review of Education*, 15 (13): 267–79.

Walkerdine, V. and Lucey, H. (1989) *Democracy in the Kitchen: Regulating Mothers and Socialising Daughters*. London: Virago.

Waller, W.W. (1932) *The Sociology of Teaching*. New York: Wiley.

Webb, R. (1993) The National Curriculum and the changing nature of topic work, *The Curriculum Journal*, 4 (2): 239–52.

Weedon, C. (1987) *Feminist Practice and Poststructuralist Theory*. London: Basil Blackwell.

White, J. (1993) What place values in the National Curriculum?, in P. O'Hear and J. White *Assessing the National Curriculum*. London: Paul Chapman.

Wilkinson, A., Davies, A. and Berrill, D. (1990) *Spoken English Illuminated*. Buckingham: Open University Press.

Woods, P. (1983) *Sociology and the School*. London: Routledge and Kegan Paul.

Woods, P. (1990) *Teacher Skills and Strategies*. Lewes: Falmer Press.

Woods, P. (1992) Symbolic interactionism: theory and method, in M.D. LeCompte, W. Millroy and J.P. Goetz (eds) *The Handbook of Qualitative Research in Education*. New York: Academic Press.

Woods, P. (1993) *Critical Events in Teaching and Learning*. London: Falmer Press.

Woods, P. (1994) Critical students: breakthroughs in learning, *International Studies in Sociology of Education*, 4 (2): 123–46.

Woods, P. (1995) *Creative Teachers in Primary Schools*. Buckingham: Open University Press.

Woods, P. and Wenham, P. (1994) Teaching, and researching the teaching of, a history topic: an experiment in collaboration, *The Curriculum Journal*, 5 (2): 133–61.

Woods, P. and Wenham, P. (1995) Politics and pedagogy: a case study in appropriation, *Journal of Education Policy*, 10 (2): 119–43.

Wragg, E. (1995) The long search for symmetry, *Times Educational Supplement*, 10 February, p. 3.

Zipes, J. (1995) A cautionary tale, *Times Educational Supplement*, 31 March, p. 14.

NAME INDEX

SUBJECT INDEX

CREATIVE TEACHERS IN PRIMARY SCHOOLS

Peter Woods

Is creative teaching still possible in English schools? Can teachers maintain and promote their own interests and beliefs as well as deliver a prescribed National Curriculum?

This book explores creative teachers' attempts to pursue *their* brand of teaching despite the changes. Peter Woods has discovered a range of strategies and adaptations to this end among such teachers, including resisting change which runs counter to their own values; appropriating the National Curriculum within their own ethos; enhancing their role through the use of others; and enriching their work through the National Curriculum to provide quality learning experiences. If all else fails, such teachers remove themselves from the system and take their creativity elsewhere. A strong theme of self-determination runs through these experiences.

While acknowledging hard realities, the book is ultimately optimistic, and a tribute to the dedication and inspiration of primary teachers.

The book makes an important contribution to educational theory, showing a range of responses to intensification as well as providing many detailed examples of collaborative research methods.

Contents

Introduction: Adapting to intensification – Resisting through collaboration: A whole-school perspective of the National Curriculum – The creative use and defence of space: Appropriation through the environment – The charisma of the critical other: Enhancing the role of the teacher – Teaching, and researching the teaching of, a history topic: An experiment in collaboration – Managing marginality: Aspects of the career of a primary school head – Self-determination among primary school teachers – References – Index.

208pp   0 335 19313 7 (paperback)   0 335 19314 5 (hardback)

BEGINNING TEACHING: BEGINNING LEARNING
IN PRIMARY EDUCATION

Janet Moyles (ed.)

- How can beginning primary teachers not only survive but enjoy their chosen career?
- What can newly qualified and student teachers do to recognize and address the many complexities of primary teaching?
- What are the issues which continually challenge both new and experienced teachers?

This book sets out to explore with beginning primary teachers, and the people who support them in schools and institutions, some of the wider issues which need to be considered when working with primary age children and how these are woven into the broad framework of teaching and teachers' own learning. Cameos and examples of classroom practice help to illustrate the many different aspects of teaching: what it is to be an effective and competent teacher; classroom processes such as planning, observation and assessment; the variety of ways in which children learn and develop thinking and skills; social interactions and support networks; equal opportunities; and 'in loco parentis' responsibilities.

Written in an accessible style, the aim throughout is to offer guidance and encouragement in the challenging and complex task of primary school teaching.

Contents
Introduction – Part 1: Teaching to learn – Do you really want to cope with thirty lively children and become an effective primary teacher? – The classroom as a teaching and learning context – Observation in the primary classroom – Competence-based teacher education – Part 2: Learning to teach – Primary children and their learning potential – Planning for learning – children's and teachers – Developing investigative thinking and skills in children – Developing thinking and skills in the arts – Developing oracy and imaginative skills in children through storytelling – Developing children's social skills in the classroom – Developing writing skills in the primary classroom – Part 3: Responsibilities, roles and relationships – Assessing, monitoring and recording children's progress and achievement – Equal opportunities in practice – Working with experienced others in the school – Primary teachers and the law – Concluding remarks – Index.

Contributors
Tim Brighouse, Martin Cortazzi, Maurice Galton, Barbara Garner, Linda Hargreaves, Jane Hislam, Morag Hunter-Carsch, Tina Jarvis, Neil Kitson, Mark Lofthouse, Sylvia McNamara, Roger Merry, Janet Moyles, Wendy Suschitzky, David Turner, Martin Wenham.

288pp   0 335 19435 4 (paperback)   0 335 19436 2 (hardback)

EDUCATING THE WHOLE CHILD
CROSS-CURRICULAR SKILLS, THEMES AND DIMENSIONS

John and Iram Siraj-Blatchford (eds)

This book approaches the 'delivery' of the cross curricular skills, themes and dimensions from a perspective emphasizing the culture of primary schools and the social worlds of children. The authors argue that the teaching of skills, attitudes, concepts and knowledge to young children should not be seen as separate or alternative objectives, but rather as complementary and essential elements of the educational process. It is the teacher's role to help children develop and build upon the understandings, skills, knowledge and attitudes which they bring with them into school. Learning for young children is a social activity where new skills and understandings are gained through interaction with both adults and with their peers. Each of the approaches outlined in the book is thus grounded in an essential respect and empathy for children and childhood as a distinct stage in life and not merely a preparation for the world of adulthood. For instance, the authors argue that responsibilities and decision-making are everyday experiences for children and that they need to be able to develop attitudes and skills which enable them to participate fully in their own social world.

Contents

Cross-curricular skills, themes and dimensions: an introduction – Little citizens: helping children to help each other – Effective schooling for all: the 'special educational needs' dimension – Racial equality education: identity, curriculum and pedagogy – 'Girls don't do bricks': gender and sexuality in the primary classroom – Children in an economic world: young children learning in a consumerist and post-industrial society – Catching them young: careers education in the primary years – Understanding environmental education for the primary classroom – Health education in the primary school: back to basics? – The place of PSE in the primary school – Index.

Contributors

John Bennett, Debra Costley, Debbie Epstein, Peter Lang, Val Millman, Lina Patel, Alistair Ross, Ann Sinclair Taylor, Iram Siraj-Blatchford, John Siraj-Blatchford, Balbir Kaur Sohal, Janice Wale.

192pp   0 335 19444 3 (paperback)   0 335 19445 1 (hardback)